"Every Christian can grow toward a more miraculous life. This book by Jason Noble is the new go-to resource for every Christian and church that wants to see God's power on a personal level. Not only devour it yourself, but get copies for the people you care about!"

Scott Hagan, president, North Central University

"Simply put, with God, *all* things are possible! *Breakthrough to Your Miracle* is moving, compelling and insightful. Jason's book will build your faith and help you to believe that God still does the impossible today."

John and Debbie Lindell, lead pastors, James River Church

"We still serve the God of breakthrough miracles! No matter how difficult or hopeless your situation looks, God can still break through! If you need a breakthrough in your life, I highly encourage you to read *Breakthrough to Your Miracle*. This book will help you understand in a very practical way your role in seeing God do the impossible in your life!"

Pastor Sam Rodriguez, president, National Hispanic Christian Leadership Conference; founder and lead pastor, New Season

"If you've ever doubted that the miracle-working God of the Bible is still performing miracles today, you're about to have your faith restored with this book. Jason shares story after story of God showing up and showing off, revealing that He is ready to blow us away as we position ourselves for a miracle. My faith has been boosted from reading this book, and I know yours will be, too!"

Michelle Watson, Ph.D., L.P.C., author, *Dad, Here's What I Really Need from You*

"When I produced John Smith's story for *The 700 Club* in 2015, I saw firsthand how Pastor Noble walked the Smith family through their miracle. With the same tenacity, Pastor Jason will unveil revelatory information on how to position yourself to receive your miracle. You will see that no matter what you're facing today, God still performs miracles and has one waiting just for you!"

Michelle Wilson, senior producer, *The 700 Club*

BREAKTHROUGH
TO YOUR
MIRACLE

BREAKTHROUGH
TO YOUR
MIRACLE

Believing God for the Impossible

JASON
NOBLE

with VINCE ANTONUCCI

Chosen

a division of Baker Publishing Group
Minneapolis, Minnesota

© 2019 by Jason Noble

Published by Chosen Books
11400 Hampshire Avenue South
Bloomington, Minnesota 55438
www.chosenbooks.com

Chosen Books is a division of
Baker Publishing Group, Grand Rapids, Michigan

Printed in the United States of America

ISBN 978-0-8007-9951-9

Library of Congress Cataloging-in-Publication Control Number: 2018055104

Unless otherwise indicated, Scripture quotations are from the Holy Bible, New International Version®. NIV®. Copyright © 1973, 1978, 1984, 2011 by Biblica, Inc.™ Used by permission of Zondervan. All rights reserved worldwide. www.zondervan.com. The "NIV" and "New International Version" are trademarks registered in the United States Patent and Trademark Office by Biblica, Inc.™

Scripture quotations identified ESV are from The Holy Bible, English Standard Version® (ESV®), copyright © 2001 by Crossway, a publishing ministry of Good News Publishers. Used by permission. All rights reserved. ESV Text Edition: 2016

Scripture quotations identified NIV1984 are from the Holy Bible, New International Version®. NIV®. Copyright © 1973, 1978, 1984 by Biblica, Inc.™ Used by permission of Zondervan. All rights reserved worldwide. www.zondervan.com

Scripture quotations identified NLT are from the *Holy Bible*, New Living Translation, copyright © 1996, 2004, 2007, 2013, 2015 by Tyndale House Foundation. Used by permission of Tyndale House Publishers, Inc., Carol Stream, Illinois 60188. All rights reserved.

Cover design by Dan Pitts

Author represented by The Gates Group

19 20 21 22 23 24 25   7 6 5 4 3 2 1

This book is dedicated to my wife, Paula Noble, and the Noble 4 (Avi, Ryan, Audree and Julia). Thank you for always believing in me, cheering me on, standing with me and always being ready for the adventure we call ministry. Thanks for always sticking in there even when the journey hasn't been easy! I love you more than words and am so thankful for you!

In addition to my immediate family, I would also like to dedicate this book to my parents. Mom and Dad, thank you for always cheering me on, teaching me about the things of God, raising me in an atmosphere where I saw you believe for the impossible, and the incredible purpose you spoke over my life.

This book is also dedicated to all the people who have believed for the impossible throughout the years in the places we have ministered. Thank you for allowing me to stand with you, be a part of your story and see God do the impossible in your life! You are also my heroes. I have watched many of you walk through incredibly difficult times and not flinch. Your faith has grown my faith. I pray that many more people will be encouraged to believe and trust God for the impossible in their lives.

Finally, this book is dedicated to the God who still does *the impossible*.

Contents

Contents

Foreword

You are probably reading this book because you or someone you know needs a breakthrough miracle. What is a breakthrough? It is the removal of an obstacle that has been restricting progress. So a breakthrough miracle is a miraculous event when something that has been standing in your way is removed.

Please remember that, no matter what impossibility you are facing, God takes impossible situations and turns them around. He still produces breakthroughs today! My prayer is that as you read this book, your hope will be restored, your faith will be elevated and you will begin to believe God to do impossible things in your life and in the lives of people around you.

As a producer, I love telling true stories—especially miracle stories that encourage people to have hope. God has provided incredible opportunities for me to share stories of miracles with the world through major Hollywood movies. I have worked on true stories like *The Pursuit of Happyness* and *Heaven Is for Real*. I produced the inspirational hit film *Miracles from Heaven* and now the movie *Breakthrough*.

Breakthrough and the book you hold in your hands were birthed out of the incredible real-life resurrection story of John

Smith. John was brought back to life after almost an hour with no pulse or oxygen when his mom, Joyce, walked into the hospital room and prayed, "Holy Spirit, I need You right now to come and breathe life back into my son!" His pulse immediately came back. But the doctors said John was brain dead. There was a one percent chance he would live overnight. And if he did live, he would most likely be severely neurologically impaired for the rest of his life.

What do you do at that point? Do you give up? Do you just accept what the doctors have told you? Or do you fight and refuse to let go of the promises God has given you? Joyce and Brian Smith and Pastor Jason Noble stood firm and held on to the scriptural principles outlined in this book. They saw one incredible miracle after another, all leading up to John's walking out of the hospital sixteen days later.

I believe God wants to do more miracles today. He wants to bring dead things back to life. What is our role when an impossibility comes along? My good friend Jason Noble will help you discover these answers and more. I want to encourage you to use this book as a guide when you are facing impossible situations.

In the process of making the movie *Breakthrough*, I have gotten to know Pastor Jason and his heart to help people experience breakthrough in the impossible situations of their lives. Through his experiences as a pastor, God has given him wisdom and insight on how to walk people through difficult times when they need a breakthrough. He has seen many miracles in his ministry, and I believe this book will help many more people experience the breakthrough power of God in their lives.

I am excited to see all that God does through this book as you position yourself for a miracle and believe Him for breakthrough.

DeVon Franklin, CEO, Franklin Entertainment

Acknowledgments

First of all, I would like to acknowledge Joyce, John and Brian Smith. We have walked through an incredible journey together. I'm amazed to see all that God has done since we received the call on January 19, 2015, that John had fallen under the ice. I'm excited to see all that God is still going to do because of this great miracle. You have truly become family to us. Thank you for allowing me to walk beside you. My life is so enriched because of you. John, I'm very proud of you and all that God is going to do in your life. We will be connected for life, and I love all of you very much.

I would also like to acknowledge the team of people who have helped me on this book, including my agent, Don Gates, my publisher, Chosen Books, and the team of people at Chosen: Kim Bangs, Ann Weinheimer, my editor, and everyone else on the Chosen/Baker team. You have made this process a joy! Especially, with the quick turnaround! You all are the best.

I would like to acknowledge my partner on this book, Pastor Vince Antonucci. Vince stepped in at the last minute and partnered with me to write this book. We had a very tight timeline, and he knocked it out of the park. I could not have done this book without Vince. I appreciate him more than words can say. I so appreciate his fresh insight and pastoral perspective. It enriches this book so much.

I would also like to acknowledge DeVon Franklin (producer of *Heaven Is for Real*, *Miracles from Heaven* and *Breakthrough*) and Pastor Sam Rodriquez. I'm thankful that God has brought these two men into my life. They have opened incredible doors for us, and are truly Holy Spirit-empowered and -anointed men. On a personal level they are genuine men of God. They are the same in private as they are in public. It's been an incredible journey. Thank you both for believing in me and allowing me to be a part of this incredible journey. Thank you for your spiritual leadership and the incredible impact your lives are making on the world. Thank you for standing beside us through this process and battling to share God's story with the world.

I also need to acknowledge all of the people who have stood with us through this journey of more than twenty years in ministry—all of the intercessors and prayer warriors who have stood by our side and were willing to stand in the gap. This army believed and prayed for miracles. I want to acknowledge all of the people also who have walked through very difficult crises and responded in incredible ways. They truly positioned themselves for miracles! You are my heroes. In the darkest moments your faith has shined.

Last and most important, I want to acknowledge God. As I write this I'm so thankful that we serve a God who loves and cares for us so much. I'm thankful that He has chosen to partner with us to see incredible things happen in our lives. I'm thankful that He cares for people who are suffering and walks beside us in the darkest moments of our lives. I'm thankful that His great love for us changes everything. I'm thankful that we can know God's heart today through His word and the fact that He wants to have a relationship with you and me! I'm thankful that He is active in our lives and doesn't remain a secret.

ONE

God Still Breaks Through

Your problem is not your problem.

I know you think it is. Whether it is a sickness that won't go away or a son who won't come back, not enough money for your family or too much fighting with your family, the wife you never seem to find or the husband you wish you could get rid of, the person lying to you or the person lying in front of you in a hospital room, clinging to life, your problem is not your problem.

Your problem is also not God.

I know that in your more honest moments you have wondered if it is. You have prayed, but He has not answered your prayers. Sometimes it doesn't seem as if He is paying attention to you at all. He is supposed to have compassion and power, so He could help, but He isn't.

But, no, God is *not* your problem.

What you need is a miracle, and what God is good at are miracles.

So, what is your problem?

You don't know how to position yourself to receive a miracle. *That* is the problem.

Picture a guy who needs a mode of transportation and is given all the parts to put together a motorcycle. What's the problem? This dude has no idea how to put the pieces together to make a motorcycle! (Personally, I would have no idea where to begin, other than to call a mechanic!)

Picture a woman who needs a fancy dessert for her dinner guests. She is given all the ingredients to make an amazing chocolate soufflé. What's the problem? She doesn't know how to mix the ingredients in a way that creates a soufflé.

Your problem is not your problem, and it is not God. God is still God and still does miracles. You just need to know how to position yourself to receive one.

Needing a Miracle

I was in my office when my wife, Paula, called and asked me to get to the hospital "right away." *Right away* is never good, so I grabbed my car keys and headed out.

It is a 45-minute drive to Cardinal Glennon Children's Hospital. I drove the whole way praying and confused. I knew something had happened with one of our church members, fourteen-year-old John Smith, but none of the details. And, until hearing Paula's tone of voice, I had no idea how serious it was.

Turns out, John and two friends had walked out onto frozen Lake Sainte Louise and the ice had given way. The other two boys were able to self-rescue. They were spotted, taken to the hospital and released. John could not crawl out. For fifteen minutes he was completely submerged. He swallowed enough lake water to fill his lungs completely. When the first responders finally reached him, he was dead. They transported him to St. Joseph Hospital West, trying desperately but unable to get a pulse.

John had been dead for over an hour when his mother, Joyce, hurried into the emergency room. The doctors had given up. Before calling the time of death they asked Joyce if she wanted to see him one last time to say goodbye.

Talk about needing a miracle.

What Is a Miracle?

You hear people use the word *miracle* quite a lot.

"It was a miracle I got to work on time."

"It was a miracle I didn't burn my mouth on that coffee."

"It was a miracle the Cubs won the World Series."

No. Those are not miracles. (Well, maybe the Cubs.) A miracle is not something unexpected or that goes against the odds. Those may be pleasant surprises, and God loves to bless us with special things, but they are not miracles.

A miracle is when God does something only God can do. It does not just defy probability; it defies explanation. Well, any explanation other than . . . God.

God created our natural world and the natural laws that govern it. A miracle happens when God chooses to reach down and intervene in the world He created. It is when God chooses for the supernatural to break through into the expected norms and routines of the natural. In the Bible, miracles are sometimes called *signs and wonders*. A miracle is a sign that points people to God and causes them to wonder about Him and His power; it stirs them to believe in and glorify Him.

Miracles in the Bible

The Old Testament starts with a miracle: God created the world out of nothing.

God was just getting started.

In the Old Testament we see God choosing repeatedly for the supernatural to break through the natural. God sent plagues, parted the Red Sea, stopped the sun, imposed leprosy, healed leprosy, gave a donkey the ability to talk, saved lives and resurrected the dead.

The New Testament starts with a miracle: God put skin on and entered the world He created as Jesus, His Son.

Jesus was just getting started.

In the New Testament we see Jesus choosing repeatedly for the supernatural to break through the natural. Jesus turned water into wine, calmed an angry sea, walked on water, fed thousands of people with just a small bit of food, healed people with physical diseases and mental illnesses, and resurrected the dead.

One of the times Jesus raised the dead is in Luke 7. Jesus was approaching a town called Nain when He saw a dead boy being carried out of the town gate. The boy was the only son of his mother, who was a widow. A large crowd was walking with her, mourning with her. When Jesus saw her, "his heart went out to her and he said, 'Don't cry.'" Jesus walked over to the coffin, touched it and said, "Young man, I say to you, get up!" The boy started breathing, then talking, then "Jesus gave him back to his mother" (verses 13–15).

Back then people were typically buried quickly after death. They did not have embalming fluids as we do, so it was a necessity. This mother had just lost her son, probably in the previous 24 hours. The shock was wearing off, and the pain was setting in.

Jesus walked up and "his heart went out to her." That is the first thing to note in this story: *Miracles happen because we have a God of compassion.*

Jesus saw this mom and He hurt for her. What is interesting is that this would have been a very common scene. It was a funeral procession. If you and I were driving on a Saturday morning and came across a hearse followed by a procession of cars, we would barely notice. What was happening in Nain that day was very ordinary, but Jesus had an extraordinary reaction. He felt the woman's pain.

When we struggle, when we suffer, God feels *our* pain. You might believe that your life is too insignificant, your problems too ordinary, that God would never notice you. You would be wrong. Jesus shows us we have a God who has compassion for you.

The second thing to note in this story: *Miracles happen because we have a God of power.* Have you ever had an emotional reaction to someone's pain, but you couldn't do anything to help? You felt bad. You would have helped if you could have, but there was nothing you could do.

Jesus felt something *and* He did something. He cared *and* He was able.

What did He do? He walked up and touched the coffin. In doing so, Jesus was crossing some boundaries. Back then there were rules about what you could and could not touch. Touching a dead body, or the piece of wood the body was on, was a strict no-no. But Jesus had compassion on this hurting mom, so He walked up to the coffin and ignored the religious policies. He reached out His fingers, made contact, and the young man breathed. Jesus' touch brought back the boy's life.

It also brought back the mother's hope. Hope has been called "oxygen for the soul." A moment earlier the boy had no oxygen, and the mom had no hope; Jesus gave new life to both of them.

When we struggle, when we suffer, God has the power to do something about it. You might feel that your situation is so dead God could never help you. You would be wrong. Jesus shows us we have a God who has power for us and can bring dead things in our lives back to life.

That day a miracle happened.

God did something only God can do. Jesus reached out, and His touch allowed the supernatural to break through into the natural. Dead people stay dead; but not if God chooses to do a miracle.

A miracle is also a sign that points people to God so they will believe in and glorify Him. That is exactly what happened in this story. Look at the result of the boy being raised that day: "They were all filled with awe and praised God. 'A great prophet has appeared among us,' they said. 'God has come to help his people.' This news about Jesus spread throughout Judea and the surrounding country" (Luke 7:16–17).

Does God Still Do Miracles?

Throughout the Old and New Testaments God does miracles. What about today? Does God still do miracles?

Many people say no. I'm not just talking about atheists and agnostics. A lot of people who go to church every Sunday struggle to believe God still does miracles.

Why? I think there are several reasons.

The Way We Think about God

People who believe in miracles believe in God.

People who don't believe in miracles may believe in God, but they believe in a God *who lacks compassion*. They have become convinced that God is not concerned with what is going on in their lives. They have bought into a lie that God does not care about them. The truth is that God loves us so much He allowed Jesus to die for us when we were His enemies. Now, as His adopted children and friends, He would do anything for us (see Romans 5:6–10). God is aware of every little thing going on in our lives (see Luke 12:7). God invites us to bring all of our cares to Him (see 1 Peter 5:7). God has the compassion to care about what we are going through and wants to act on our behalf, but people who don't believe in miracles doubt that.

People who don't believe in miracles may believe in God, but they believe in a God *who lacks power.* They may or may not believe the stories in the Bible that demonstrate God's power, but they have become convinced that God does not have, or refuses to use, that kind of power today.

There are a lot of people in our world who know about God, but they do not truly know Him. Second Timothy 3:5 tells us that some people have the appearance of godliness but deny its power. You can know about God, but if you have never experienced His life-changing power you don't really know Him.

The truth is that God is the same yesterday, today and forever (see Hebrews 13:8). God did not stop being God when the Bible stopped being written. God has not changed and has not lost His power.

The Way We Think about Life

Why do people, even those who go to church and say they believe in God, not believe in miracles? I think for some it's the way they want to approach life.

There was a time when people were comfortable with mystery and unpredictability. It was kind of necessary because there was so much we did not understand. Today, at least in America, people feel as though they have it all figured out. Rather than being small cogs in a big universe, many feel like masters of the universe—anti-supernatural, fiercely independent, self-reliant and wanting to be in control. That doesn't leave much room for God to do something unpredictable.

In the beginning, God made humans the way He wanted them to be. I wonder if we have returned the favor? Many people are not interested in a God who can intervene in their lives. They feel threatened if He works in ways they cannot control.

The Way We Want Others to Think about Us

Pastor Craig Groeschel talks about Christians who believe in God but live as if He doesn't exist, calling them "Christian atheists."[1]

A couple of decades earlier, Stanley Hauerwas, professor of theological ethics at Duke University Divinity School, and William H. Willimon, professor of Christian ministry at Duke, wrote an article in *Christian Century* in which they gave the same assessment of Christians: "The central problem for our church, its theology, and its ethics is that it is simply atheistic."[2] The title of their article is interesting: "Embarrassed by God's Presence."

I think that is another issue that keeps people from believing in miracles. It is not just the way we think about God and life; it is also the way we want others to think about us. It seems to me that Christians want to be known, more than anything else, for being *normal*. In Bible times we see Christians known for their great love, for living sacrificial lives and for the miracles God did among them.[3] There was nothing normal about them. That is why people were so amazed by them.

Today, many Christians worry about seeming "weird." They don't want to be different; they want to be respectable. If you want to be normal, miracles do not really fit into your theology or way of life.

God Is Still in the Miracle Business

People may struggle to believe, but God is still in the miracle business. He has not lost His compassion or power. What He was capable of then, He is capable of now. What used to happen still happens.

You can believe that in faith, or you can believe that because of the evidence. In fact, most people who train a skeptical eye on the theology and the real-life claims regarding miracles usually come to believe that they are true.

C. S. Lewis, a former atheist, studied what the Bible says about miracles and whether or not miracles still happen. He focused on theology and philosophical arguments. His conclusion? God is still in the miracle business. Lewis wrote a book proving miracles still happen that he titled *Miracles*.[4]

Craig Keener, another former non-believer, traveled the world investigating claims of modern miracles. His conclusion? God is still in the miracle business. He wrote a (more than 1,200-page!) two-volume book proving miracles still happen that he titled *Miracles*.[5]

Eric Metaxas, another former skeptic, analyzed the topic of miracles, questioning whether or not miracles and science can coexist. Metaxas writes, "The idea that science is somehow at odds with faith and miracles is false. It's actually not only false but also demonstrably illogical."[6] Metaxas's conclusion? God is still in the miracle business. He wrote a book proving miracles still happen that he titled *Miracles*.

Lee Strobel, a Pulitzer Prize–winning journalist, and another former atheist, used his investigative skills to determine whether or not miracles are still happening. Part of his investigation involved interviews with atheists who made the best possible arguments against God and the supernatural. Strobel's conclusion? God is still in the miracle business. He wrote a book proving miracles still happen that he titled *The Case for Miracles*.[7] (At least he added a few words to the *Miracles* title!)

God still does miracles. Even skeptics have been convinced.

But the big question is this: Are you? Do you believe?

It is a big question because whether or not you believe God can do a miracle may well be the difference between whether or not you receive one.

That brings us back to the emergency room in St. Louis.

Resurrection

John had been dead for over an hour. No pulse, no oxygen.

Joyce walked into the room, saw her son's lifeless body, and cried out with a voice that could be heard throughout the emergency room, "I believe in a God who can do miracles! Holy Spirit, I need You right now to come and breathe life back into my son!"

Immediately, the EKG monitors started to beep. John had a pulse. He was breathing.

The doctors were shocked. John was alive. But he was still facing desperate circumstances, so they decided to airlift him to Cardinal Glennon.

I arrived at Cardinal Glennon and was stunned to see the Pediatric Intensive Care Unit (PICU) waiting room overflowing with friends, family, church members, classmates; all of them there for John.

People updated me in hushed tones. Forty-five minutes of resuscitation efforts could not raise a pulse. *Nothing* could get a pulse. He was not breathing. His heart was not beating. John was dead. Joyce walked in, prayed and he came back to life.

As I was talking with people in the waiting room, John's parents, Joyce and Brian, walked out of their meeting with the doctor. Brian had arrived shortly after Joyce. Joyce told us what the doctors had told them. John was brain dead. All of his organs were in catastrophic failure. They gave John a one percent chance of making it through the night. If he did make it, he would be a "vegetable."

We decided that we were not giving up. We believed in a miracle-working God and trusted that He was going to break through.

I took a group of pastors into John's room, and we started to pray. Over the next weeks we continued to pray.

As we prayed, God did miracle after miracle. John made it through the first night. He woke up on the third day. He had the ventilator taken out on the seventh day. John walked out of the hospital on the sixteenth day. On the fortieth day he was completely cleared by his doctors. At this writing nearly four years later, he is a fully healthy young man.

Even doctors who did not believe in miracles called it a miracle.[8]

What Miracle Are You Seeking?

God is a God of compassion and power. God loves us, is for us and wants to come through for us. A God-sized problem requires a God-sized solution and creates a moment for God to break through. God is willing and able to intervene and do miracles because He loves us and wants to reveal Himself to us. He did miracles throughout the Old and New Testaments, and He is still doing them today. I saw John Smith raised from the dead, and I have seen many others. I will be sharing a bunch with you.

But *you* are the one I am wondering about.

I wonder why you are reading this book. Perhaps you are facing an impossible situation and you are looking for a miracle. Where do you need God to intervene? Maybe . . .

You have received a scary diagnosis from a doctor.

You are not sure if your marriage is going to make it.

Since you were a kid, the only way you've communicated with your mother was through yelling, and you want finally to move past that.

You are battling an addiction, and you never experience victory.

Your finances are a disaster, and you have no idea what to do.

A loved one is going through chemo, and the situation is not looking promising.

You have never been able to forgive the person who abused you.

You cannot stop overeating or overspending.

People you care about have no interest in Jesus; you can't get through to them.

You worry incessantly and know it shows a lack of faith.

You hate your job but are afraid to launch out on a new career path.

You have been struggling with the same debilitating condition for years.

The son or daughter you love has walked away from God, and there is no sign of a return.

You have low self-esteem, and it is killing you.

So, do you believe God can do what you need Him to do?

But Will He Do It for You?

God does miracles. Still.

So, why don't we see more of them today?

Why are *you* not experiencing a miracle when you are so desperate for one?

Those are good questions, important questions. Throughout my years of studying the Bible and interacting with thousands of people through my role as a pastor, I have discovered something: It is no coincidence that certain people do not receive the miracles they hope for and certain people do.

You might guess that I have found this difference between them: Some people *lack* faith for miracles; other people *have* faith for miracles; some people believe God *can*; other people believe God *will*.

That is part of it but not all of it.

It turns out that people who receive miracles don't just receive miracles; they *position* themselves to receive miracles.

When Joyce Smith walked into that room, her son was dead; but that was not her problem. Her problem was positioning herself for a miracle. Because Joyce trusts in the God who can raise the dead, she knew how to position herself to receive the miracle she needed.

Your problem is not your problem, and God is not your problem. God is still God and still does miracles. You just need to know how to position yourself to receive one.

I wrote this book to help you know how to position yourself so you can break through to your miracle. God longs to intervene in your life and do for you what cannot otherwise be done. He has the compassion and the power. He is ready and eager to move on your behalf. He is inviting you to position yourself to partner with Him and make the impossible possible. Let's position ourselves so God can show up, show off and draw people to Himself.

CONNECT WITH GOD

God, thank You for loving me. Thank You that You care about me and what is going on in my life. You know me, and You know I have moments of doubt. But God, I believe You are who You say You are and can do what You say You can do. I am facing some situations that seem impossible, but I know that nothing is impossible for You, and that the impossible is nothing to You. I am so grateful that You want to be a part of my life. God, please grow my belief. Teach me how to position myself for a miracle. I thank You in advance for the miracles I believe You will do in my life, and I pray they all bring You glory. In Jesus' name, Amen.

POSITION YOURSELF

1. Read the healing miracles in the New Testament that Jesus performed. Write down the practical things you see people did before and after Jesus healed them.

2. What impossible situations do you need God to break through for you? Write them down, and keep track of everything God does. Watch for the little things that might not seem like miracles.

3. Commit to praying every day for the miracles you are seeking, believing that your breakthrough is coming.

GROUP DISCUSSION QUESTIONS

1. What do you truly believe about God and His ability to do miracles in your life?

2. What past events and circumstances have shaped your perspective on miracles?

3. Where do you need God's breakthrough in your life?

4. Do you really believe that God loves you enough to step in and do miracles in your life? Why or why not?

5. What is keeping you from believing that God can do a miracle in your situation?

6. What is the next step you need to take after reading this chapter?

TWO

Play Your Part

Jeff Markin was a 53-year-old auto mechanic. He didn't feel good, drove to Palm Beach Gardens (Florida) Hospital, walked into the emergency room and dropped dead from a heart attack. Doctors tried for forty minutes but could not revive him.

Supervising cardiologist Chauncey Crandall came in to examine the body. Markin's toes, fingers and face had turned black. His eyes were open with dilated, fixed pupils. At 8:05 p.m. Dr. Crandall declared him dead.

Markin's story, however, was not over, and Dr. Crandall had a part to play.

Why?

First of all, why did Jeff Markin die? Why didn't God save him? If God still does miracles today, might He not have slipped in a quick healing there? Jeff Markin likely was loved by people who needed him and would miss him. Why didn't God do something?

We all have those "Why didn't God do something?" stories. We have all asked that question.

I am going to tell you my answer, and it may not sit well with you. Here it is: I don't think it is God; I think it is *us*. I believe we have a part to play for miracles to happen, and if we fail to fulfill our part, we are responsible for the miracle *not* happening. We blame God. But maybe, if there is blame to assign, we need to point the finger at ourselves.

You might be asking, "Are you saying that we can inhibit the work of God?" God is all powerful. Certainly, you are not saying we can shut down the work of God.

God *is* all powerful, but, yes, I am saying we can shut down the work of God. How can I say that? Because the Bible says that. Remember when Jesus went to His hometown? What happened? "And because of their unbelief, he couldn't do any miracles among them except to place his hands on a few sick people and heal them. And he was amazed at their unbelief" (Mark 6:5–6 NLT).

Also, why do we see Jesus not just healing people, but first asking, "Do you believe I can do this?" (see Matthew 9:28)? And why did Jesus tell people, "Your faith has healed you" (Luke 18:42)?

Jesus not only asked for, or perhaps even required, faith; He also often asked people to participate in the needed miracle in some way.

God Works Through Us

Jesus' first recorded miracle is changing water to wine at a wedding. The miracle starts with a crisis. In fact, *every* miracle starts with a crisis. We need to see and acknowledge it.

Jesus was at a wedding reception. (I love it that Jesus was invited to parties!) He was enjoying the festivities with His mom,

His disciples and the other partygoers. The crisis happened when, in the middle of the party, the hosts ran out of wine. That might not sound like a big deal to us, but it was a disaster for a family throwing a party in Jesus' day. It indicated bad hospitality and was humiliating for the hosts.

They ran out of wine, and Mary found out. Look at how she handled the problem.

> When the wine was gone, Jesus' mother said to him, "They have no more wine."
>
> "Woman, why do you involve me?" Jesus replied. "My hour has not yet come."
>
> His mother said to the servants, "Do whatever he tells you."
>
> Nearby stood six stone water jars, the kind used by the Jews for ceremonial washing, each holding from twenty to thirty gallons.
>
> Jesus said to the servants, "Fill the jars with water"; so they filled them to the brim.
>
> Then he told them, "Now draw some out and take it to the master of the banquet."
>
> They did so, and the master of the banquet tasted the water that had been turned into wine. He did not realize where it had come from, though the servants who had drawn the water knew. Then he called the bridegroom aside and said, "Everyone brings out the choice wine first and then the cheaper wine after the guests have had too much to drink; but you have saved the best till now."
>
> What Jesus did here in Cana of Galilee was the first of the signs through which he revealed his glory; and his disciples believed in him.
>
> John 2:3–11

Did you notice *how* Jesus did the miracle? He did it *through people*. When Jesus decided to change the water to wine He could have just . . . said the word or . . . wrinkled His nose like that lady on *Bewitched* or . . . blinked His eyes like that lady on *I Dream of Jeannie* or . . . anything. But Jesus chose to do the miracle through people. He told the servers to fill the serving jars with water. He had them dip some of the wine out and take it to the master of ceremonies. Jesus used people. They had a part to play in the miracle.

It reminds me of when Jesus miraculously fed five thousand hungry people.[1] Back in the beginning, God created the world *ex nihilo. Ex nihilo* means "out of nothing." It would have been nothing for Jesus to create thousands of lunches out of nothing. Jesus has all the power in the world, and certainly enough power to do this miracle all by Himself. But yet He asked the disciples to find some food . . . then had a boy donate his Happy Meal . . . and then directed the disciples to hand out the food to the crowds. Jesus used people. They had a part to play in the miracle.

Jesus told us that we would have a part to play in miracles:

> "I tell you the truth, anyone who believes in me will do the same works I have done, and even greater works, because I am going to be with the Father. You can ask for anything in my name, and I will do it, so that the Son can bring glory to the Father. Yes, ask me for anything in my name, and I will do it!"
>
> John 14:12–14 NLT

When we partner with God and align our will with His, He will answer our prayers, and we will see Him do even greater works through us!

When Jesus performs miracles, He calls on us to be part of the miracle. We play an important role in God's work. He chooses to work through us, whether the crisis is ours or someone else's.

God wants heaven to invade earth, and He lets us be the conduits through which that happens. He puts His power into play in the crises we face *through us*. God does not do miracles without human partnership. We need to position ourselves. We have a responsibility to play our part.

Think of a baseball player out in the field. He can't make the batter hit the ball to him. He does not have that kind of power or control. But he *must* be ready. He has to position himself and be prepared to catch the ball if it is hit to him. If he is not ready, he will miss it.

In the same way, we cannot make miracles happen. We do not have that kind of power or control. God is the only miracle worker. But God chooses to use people when He performs miracles. That means we have to be ready. We have to be positioned and prepared to play our part. If we are not, we will miss it.

We have a part to play. What part?

Believe

Two blind men asked Jesus to heal them (see Matthew 9:27–31). Jesus did not immediately heal them. Instead, He asked, "Do you believe I can do this?"

The men replied, "Yes, Lord."

Then Jesus healed them. The men had a part to play that went beyond merely wanting a miracle; Jesus asked them to believe.

What precipitated Jesus' turning the water into wine? The miracle happened only because Mary went to Jesus, believing He could solve the crisis. If Mary had not gone to Jesus in faith, the miracle would not have happened.

When crisis hits, you go to Jesus. Like Mary, you tell Him about it, and you believe He will solve it. Realize that the real issue is *spiritual*, not physical. That can be hard to do, because what we see is a physical need. But we are assured in the Bible that our true battle is against the spiritual forces of darkness, which seek to wreak havoc in our lives to get us distracted and pull us away from God. At its heart, your crisis (whether it is your kid who won't behave, your boss who isn't fair or your marriage that isn't healthy) is *spiritual*. Recognize that and go to Jesus. Tell Him what is wrong and know that He will fix it.

Obey

Mary believed that Jesus could do something about the wine shortage. She went to Jesus, then commanded the servers: "Do whatever He tells you."

Mary did not tell Jesus how to solve the problem. She trusted Him for the outcome, but she did not dictate the method. When you need a miracle, don't tell God, "Here is exactly what You have to do." Instead, trust Him with the outcome and ask Him, "What do You want *me* to do?"

Mary told the servers, "Do whatever He tells you," and they did. As commanded, they filled the jars with water and took some to the master of the ceremony. As they obeyed, the miracle happened.

Your part is to *believe* and *obey*. Positioning yourself for a miracle includes believing and obeying whatever God tells you to do.

A Miracle *Through* You

It may be that God wants to do a miracle *through* you. Will He? It depends. *Do you believe and will you obey?* You need to have awareness that crises are spiritual in nature. You need to ask God, "What do You want me to do?" And you need to obey what He tells you.

I walked into Costco one day and saw a woman I know. I said, "Hey! How are you doing?"

She put on a brave smile and then said, "Honestly, I've had a horrible migraine for four days."

I frowned. "I'm so sorry, I'll pray for you." (That's what pastors say. I think *I'll pray for you* is on the official pastor business card.) I walked away, intent on doing my shopping and getting out as fast as I could.

As I went down the aisle, God stopped me. *Jason, what are you doing? You said you were going to pray for her. You are not going to pray for her. You go pray for her right now.*

I realized God was right. (I know, I know. God is *always* right.) But I was also in a hurry, and, besides, I thought it might be awkward to return to the woman now. But I want to obey God— all the time, immediately and no matter what excuses I have for disobedience. So I turned around, went back and said, "I'm sorry. I'd actually like to pray for you right now, right here. May I do that?"

She agreed and I prayed and I said, "Amen," and she said the migraine was gone.

It hit me: God wanted to do a miracle in that woman's life, but God doesn't do miracles without human partnership. For the miracle to happen, I had to play my part. I had to be ready and willing to believe and obey.

A Miracle *in* You

Or it may be that God wants to do a miracle *in* you. Will He? Again, it depends. *Do you believe and will you obey?*

I think of the guy we meet at a pool in the fifth chapter of John's gospel. This guy was paralyzed, stuck lying on a mat for 38 years.

Jesus approached him and asked, "Do you want to get well?"

It seems like an odd question. Of course he wanted to get well, right? Well, maybe not. Sometimes people can get used to being sick. Some enjoy being the victim. In fact, it can become their identity. Some have grown reliant on getting pity and help from others. Jesus asked if he wanted to get well, and it was a good question.

Do *you* want to get well? You have been plagued with whatever you have been plagued with for a while, but do you *really* want to get well? Every miracle starts with a crisis. We have to see and acknowledge the crisis, *and* we have to want to get well.

Next, Jesus told the man, "Pick up your mat and walk." For you or me, to pick up a mat and walk is easy. But that was the one thing this man could not do. For 38 years he had been unable to stand, to pick up a mat or to walk. As much as he might have wanted to, everything in him must have screamed, *I can't do what He is asking me to do!*

It would take faith for him to believe he was now capable of doing what he knew he could not do. The moment of truth hovered: Would the man obey what Jesus was commanding?

The same is true today. If you see and acknowledge a crisis in your life or someone else's, you need to position yourself for a miracle. You believe Jesus can solve it, and you ask Him, "What do You want me to do?" Then, as Mary told the servers, "Do whatever He tells you."

In his book *The Case for Miracles*, Lee Strobel tells of a woman whose leg was paralyzed. She was given no hope of recovery. But after a priest prayed for her, she had a vision of God telling her to stand up and walk. She obeyed—and was completely healed.[2]

That sounds a lot like what happened with the man at the pool in John 5. This is no surprise. God is the same yesterday, today and forever; He is still in the miracle business. Jesus told us to pray that what is true in heaven will be true on earth. God wants to invade earth with heaven, and we are the conduits He wants to use. God longs to do amazing things in our lives, but we have a part to play. To position ourselves for a miracle we have to believe and obey.

Father God, I Cry Out

The heart attack had killed Jeff Markin.

Dr. Crandall filled out the report and had started to leave when he had a compelling sense that God was telling him to go back and pray for the dead man. Cardiologists do not pray for corpses. Crandall thought the idea was foolish, not to mention embarrassing. He continued on his way out, but again felt God prompting him to turn around.

He obeyed, reluctantly.

A nurse was sponging the dead body in preparation for it to be sent to the morgue.

Dr. Crandall began praying over the corpse, "Father God, I cry out for the soul of this man. Please raise him from the dead right now in Jesus' name."

At his direction, the dead body was then hooked up to a monitor and shocked with paddles. Instantly the reading went from flat line to a healthy 75 beats per minute.

Markin began breathing without assistance. His color returned. Markin was restored to full health.[3]

What miracle does God want to do *through* you?

Is there a miracle God wants to do *in* you?

Do you believe? And will you obey?

CONNECT WITH GOD

Father God, You did miracles when the servers obeyed Jesus, when the little boy gave his lunch to Jesus, when the man at the pool believed and did what Jesus asked him to do. It is amazing to me that not only do You love me, and not only do You forgive my sins, but also You want to use me to do great things in the world. I want to be the conduit through which You release Your power and do Your work here on earth. Please help me to do my part. Help me to believe and obey. Thank You. I pray in Jesus' name, Amen.

POSITION YOURSELF

1. Why do you think God chooses to do miracles through people? Look back over your life: How has God used you to bring heaven to earth? How has He answered your prayers? What impact has He made through you? Thank Him!

2. What miracle do you think God might want to do *through* you? In whose life or what situation are you positioned to be a conduit through which God does something amazing? In that place, have you positioned yourself for God to do a miracle through you? Have you recognized and acknowledged the crisis? Have you taken it to Jesus? Do you believe He can solve it? Have you asked Him what He wants you to do? Have you obeyed? Talk to God about all of that. Pray for His help.

3. What miracle do you think God might want to do *in* you? What issue has been plaguing your life for a long time, or what crisis has hit your life recently? Whatever it is, have

you positioned yourself for God to do a miracle through you? Have you recognized and acknowledged the crisis? Have you taken it to Jesus? Do you believe He can solve it? Have you asked Him what He wants you to do? Have you obeyed? Talk to God about all of that. Pray for His help.

GROUP DISCUSSION QUESTIONS

1. What do you think is your responsibility when it comes to seeing a miracle happen?
2. How can you play your part in the miracle you are seeking?
3. A key ingredient to positioning yourself for a miracle is belief. Do you really believe that God can do miracles? Why or why not?
4. Is there a situation where you prayed and believed God for a miracle, but the result was not what you expected? What did that do to your belief?
5. What really spoke to you in this chapter? What impact will it have on how you position yourself for a miracle?

THREE

Get Close to Jesus

She is desperate. She has spent every last bit of money searching for a cure to her disease. For twelve years she has hemorrhaged. It has been twelve years of pain and anguish, of being labeled unclean and being avoided. She has paid every dollar she has to every doctor she can find, but she only gets worse. And now she is left with no money and little hope.

At the brink of despair, she hears about one final option. A man people claim is a miracle worker, a true healer. Could the stories about this man actually be true?

I assume that as a young Jewish girl she would have been taught about God and how He helps the hurting. She would have heard these words from Scripture: "Under his wings you will find refuge" (Psalm 91:4). She would have learned of God's promise to send a Messiah to rescue His people. And she must surely have taken these words of Malachi to heart: "For you who fear my name, the Sun of Righteousness will rise with healing in his wings" (Malachi 4:2 NLT). A Messiah was coming, and this "Sun of Righteousness" would have healing in His wings.

Could this man she is hearing about be the Messiah her people are waiting for?

She has to find out.

The Journey

I can imagine that her journey to Jesus is difficult for many reasons. She is weak and tired. It's my understanding that she has to travel a good distance to meet up with Him, and she has no transportation. Because of her sickness she is considered unclean and cursed by God; no one will offer to help her for fear of touching her.

So, she sets out on foot, alone. Her mind probably taunts her as she leans against a tree to get shade and rest, or as she waits for a drink from a well at night after the crowds have gone. *What a stupid thing—to have hope based on a rumor! Do you really think you can be healed? After all these years? After all you've gone through? You need to give up and accept your fate. Just turn back and go home.*

"No," she says with new determination. "I will find this man. And He *will* heal me."

Finally, after crossing the miles, she finds Him. It's easy to spot Him; it seems as if the entire town is crowding around Him. People are all pressing in on Him, perhaps shouting their needs at Him, trying to get close.

She stands back and considers the situation. How can she get to Him? She is a social outcast. She can't squeeze her way through the crowd without touching people. If they notice her, they can haul her away or even kill her.

Close Enough to Touch

But He is her only hope. This is her last chance.

I can't turn back now, she thinks. *I won't turn back now. I'm not giving up until I'm healed.*

But the crowds. How can she get to Him?

She has no other choice; she has to get close to Jesus. She encourages herself with a thought: *If I only touch His cloak, I will be healed.*

You might wonder: Why does she think touching His clothes will be enough? Remember that verse about the Messiah having healing "in His wings"? That verse was written in Hebrew, and the Hebrew word for *wing* is *kanaph*. *Kanaph* is also the word for the corner of a garment. She must have taken the ancient prophecy to mean that the Messiah would have healing in His *kanaph*.

If this man is the Messiah, all she has to do is touch the corner of His cloak.

Determination renewed, she steps into the crowd and bravely pushes her way toward the middle. She sees Him. His back is toward her. Perfect. She reaches out her hand *stretching . . . stretching . . . stretching.* She extends her fingers, trying to get them a little closer. Finally, they brush the edge of His cloak.

Immediately, the strangest sensation flows through her body. A tingling warmth. She knows instantly.

She has been healed. She has gotten close to Jesus, and she has been healed.

Pouring Out Everything

Now, she believes, it is time to get *away* from Jesus, to sneak away from the crowd before anyone recognizes her.

Then she hears Jesus' voice. He is announcing rather loudly that someone has just touched Him and has been healed. She freezes. The people with Jesus tell Him that with so many in the crowd, *lots* of people are touching Him. She breathes a sigh of relief and takes another step away. But Jesus says no, lots of people are touching Him, but only *one* person touched Him with faith that took healing power out of Him. She realizes she cannot go unnoticed. "Then the woman, knowing what had happened to her, came and fell at his feet and, trembling with fear, told him the whole truth" (Mark 5:33).

This is *not* part of her plan, but she comes forward and tells Jesus *everything*. She is honest with Him about her problem.

I think that is critical, not just for her, but for *us*. In fact, I'm not sure we can get the miracle we seek without bringing Jesus the whole truth. In the Bible we learn that God heals what we reveal but cannot heal what we conceal.[1] If you want healing, move close to Jesus and tell Him the whole truth. Tell Him what has happened, what you have done, how you are hurting, what you need from Him.

That's what she does. She tells Jesus the whole truth. Then she waits.

Outcast or Daughter?

She is terrified because she doesn't know what is about to happen. She *does* know that she has broken the law by coming into contact with the crowd. She *does* know she has made this rabbi unclean by touching Him.

She *does not* know that the situation is even worse than she imagines. Jesus is making His way to the house of a rich man named Jairus, whose little daughter is dying. Jairus is a synagogue ruler. That makes him important. He has status and respect. We also know he has money, because we are told he has servants. He is a *somebody*.

This woman is *not*.

We know Jairus's name. We don't know hers. She is anonymous.

Jairus is a synagogue ruler; she is not allowed to enter the synagogue because her sickness makes her unclean. In fact, back then people thought if you were sick you were cursed by God. Jairus is considered a holy man; she is considered unclean *and* sinful.

Jairus is rich. She has no money; she has spent it all on doctors.

Jairus is a somebody. She is a nobody.

If she knew that Jesus was on His way to help Jairus, she would be even *more* afraid of what Jesus is about to say to her.

So, what does He say? He says, "Daughter, your faith has healed you. Go in peace."

Wow!

This is the only time in Scripture that Jesus calls someone by the term of endearment *daughter*.

Jesus pushes *pause* on Jairus and the miracle he is seeking, to give His full attention to this woman. He interrupts His time with a somebody to be with a nobody. Why? Because with Jesus, nobodies are somebodies.

Peace

Jesus calls her to come forward in front of the whole crowd—the very thing she does not want to do—and He tells her that her faith has healed her and that she can go in peace.

Why?

Why doesn't Jesus let her sneak away as she wants? Why does Jesus compel her to come to Him?

Because He knows it is not just her body that needs to be restored. She also has to be restored *to her community*. She needs people to know that she is no longer sick, no longer unclean. She needs everyone to know that Jesus, the sinless one, does not consider her sinful. He calls her *daughter*, tells her she can go and live in peace.

Everyone in the crowd hears. Word starts spreading.

Jesus heals her, not only physically but also emotionally and relationally. He heals her in every way she needs to be healed.

That is what Jesus wants to do for you. That is what happens when faith drives you to get close to Him.

No Plan B

This woman was desperate. She had tried every plan imaginable, but no plan would work. She was out of plans, until she heard about Jesus. He then became plan A. She had no plan B.

Her plan: Get close to Jesus.

That was pretty much the extent of it. Get close to Jesus. Even if it meant a journey in her weak condition. Get close to Jesus.

Once she got close to Jesus, the next phase of the plan came into focus: Get *closer* to Jesus. Even if it meant pushing through a crowd of people she was forbidden to touch. Get closer to Jesus.

One she got closer, she realized the only way to bring her plan to a successful completion: Get *even closer* to Jesus. Even if it meant reaching out and touching someone she was not allowed to touch. Get even closer to Jesus.

Her plan worked. She got close to Jesus, and her life was changed in an instant.

Had she stayed home, wallowing in her sickness, stuck in self-pity, she would have died, alone, in her disease. But she walked out of her past and into her future by getting close to Jesus.

She positioned herself for a miracle, and God broke through.

Paula

God has blessed me with an amazing wife. Paula is an incredible partner in ministry and parenting.

Paula was a very broken girl when I first met her. The enemy had worked overtime to convince her she was not good enough, not wanted and not loved.

Paula's mom was in her late thirties when she found out she was pregnant with Paula. She already had five children. Her husband was an alcoholic, and she feared what he would say when he found out.

Abortion had just been legalized, and the doctor offered her a way out of this unplanned pregnancy. Paula's mom decided that abortion would be the best solution for everyone and agreed to have her doctor make the arrangements. Paula's mom had a relationship with Jesus, but she just didn't see any other way. A few days passed while she was awaiting the appointment details. During that time God spoke very clearly to her. She sensed Him saying that the child she was carrying was His plan. He had a purpose for that baby. She knew she could not have the abortion and decided it was time to tell her husband about the pregnancy. That was another disaster. He didn't believe the baby was his and told her he wasn't raising another child.

Paula's mom finally decided that the only way to move forward was to leave her husband. She took her kids and moved back home to Oregon to be near family. Her family would end up living in a one-bedroom shack with no hot water and no bathroom. They scraped by as Paula's mom did her best to take care of six kids. Her family did have a bright spot. They loved each other very much.

Paula learned about the near abortion when she was fourteen, and it crushed her to find out. She already felt unwanted because her dad was absent; this felt like more proof.

When Paula was a young girl she was sexually molested by someone in her church. This reinforced her sense that she was worthless.

Paula's mom remarried and this new stepfather made Paula's life miserable. He made clear repeatedly that she wasn't wanted.

Finally, Paula's senior year of high school arrived, and she hoped her real father would show up for her graduation. She was told he would, and she believed this would change everything. He did show up, drunk. Paula's heart broke.

Once again, the enemy whispered to her that she was worthless, that no one wanted her.

Paula was the first member of her family to go to college. She even went on to get her master's degree. It was impressive, but it was driven by Paula's need to prove that she was worth something.

We got married during college. As we prepared for the wedding she was continually reminded that her dad would not be walking her down the aisle. We were thankful that Paula has an incredible brother-in-law who stepped in. Paula's dad showed up for the wedding but, again, completely drunk. He didn't even talk to her.

As we began our marriage, we struggled. Paula wanted to run away from confrontation or hard conversations. She was always very guarded. I did not realize until much later how much hurt was in her heart.

She needed a miracle. God needed to heal her broken heart and help her release the bitterness she was holding on to. She needed to find her identity in God, that she was wanted and loved by Him. But her walls of self-protection were so high I didn't think she would let anyone break through, including me, or even God.

Her pain continued to grow worse when, first, her aunt died, then her dad died due to alcohol, then her brother passed away due to alcohol as well.

Paula compensated for her pain and for her lack of self-worth by overachieving and being self-reliant.

Increasingly, I could see how burdened Paula was, and I began to pray. I asked friends to pray for her.

God heard our prayers.

God breaks through. He does miracles, and He wants to heal not only our bodies, but our spirits and our souls as well. That is what He had in store for Paula.

Paula began to realize that the idea of having a loving heavenly Father had no meaning for her, because she really had no understanding of what having a loving father was like. She finally understood that even though she went to church every week, she was running away from God, not to Him. She was afraid to trust God as her Father. She decided it was time to run into the arms of Jesus.

The process took a year. Paula kept growing closer to Jesus, and He began showing her areas of her life that He wanted to heal.

She had to forgive her dad. It was challenging. Forgiveness is like an onion. You didn't get hurt just once; you have to let God take you through your hurt, one layer at a time. As she worked toward forgiving, Paula realized Jesus also wanted to take away the shame she was carrying.

Paula pushed through, getting closer and closer to Jesus, and God healed her from the inside out. It was truly a miracle. God was able to break down her walls and set her free.

Get Close to Jesus

The woman we read about in Scripture and my wife are separated by about two thousand years and seven thousand miles, but they both found the exact same solution: Get close to Jesus. The solution for *whatever* we are going through is Jesus, getting close to Jesus. We need to follow the example of these women.

Belief That Brings You Close

For the woman we met in the Bible, faith is what led her to get close to Jesus. She believed enough to make, very likely, a trek of many miles. When she hit the wall of a crowd that stood between her and Jesus, she pushed herself forward with words of faith: *If I only touch His cloak, I will be healed.* How did she come to that faith? We don't know the details, but faith came from hearing about Jesus. She heard stories of His healing power and had probably heard the prophecies about Him in the Old Testament when she was young.

Faith is *always* what leads someone to get close to Him. Without faith, we are not going to get to Jesus, we are not going to look to Jesus, and we are not going to be positioned for a miracle.

The Bible tells us that "faith comes from hearing, that is, hearing the Good News about Christ" (Romans 10:17 NLT). Faith comes from hearing about Jesus. As our faith grows, we want to get close to Him. As we get close to Jesus, we are positioning ourselves for a miracle.

Since you are reading this book, I'm guessing that at some point you started believing in Jesus. What are you doing to grow your belief? I don't know your story, but I do know that faith always comes from hearing. How are you hearing about Jesus? Are you in church every week? Do you read your Bible every day? Do you listen to worship music? Do you have friends who talk about Jesus? Do you seek out stories of Jesus doing the impossible to grow your belief that He can do what's impossible for you?

On the morning John Smith fell through the ice, his mother, Joyce, was having her daily Bible study. She was using a devotional book by Beth Moore called *Believing God*. No wonder a couple hours later she walked into the emergency room believing God is who He said He is and can do what He says He can do!

When you face something awful, will you believe that? You think you will, but will you *really*? The answer depends on how much you have been hearing about Jesus.

Pushing Through to Get Close

The woman in the Bible had faith that made her want to get close to Jesus, but it turned out to be more challenging than she anticipated.

She had been sick so long she probably struggled to have hope that change could ever happen.

She had to take the long journey alone.

Doubts must have crept in. Would she find Him? Would Jesus even want to help her if she did?

She made progress. And then she faced a wall of people who made it seem impossible to get close enough to Jesus to get the miracle she was seeking.

I wonder. What will *you* have to push through to get to Jesus?

Brad Wilkinson, an eight-year-old boy, had two holes in his heart. Like the woman in the Bible, he was literally leaking blood. To get to Jesus, Brad had to push past his dad's unbelief. Ed Wilkinson, educated in neuropsychology, was convinced that people who turn to Jesus just use faith as a crutch because they can't deal with reality.

When surgery was scheduled for Brad, he asked his father, "Am I going to die?"

His father could only say that it was possible.

Brad asked, "Can Jesus heal me?"

After careful thought, Ed said that God does heal, but he didn't know if God would.

Soon after that, a pastor asked Brad, "Do you believe that Jesus can heal you?" Brad pushed past his father's lack of faith and said yes.

The pastor prayed for him.

The day of the surgery, after Brad was taken for preparation, the surgeon unexpectedly entered the waiting room and asked Ed to come with him. He showed Ed two videos of Brad's heart.

One, taken the day before, showed blood leaking from one chamber to another. The second, taken just before surgery was to begin, showed a wall where the leak had been. There was no need for surgery.

The surgeon said, "You can count this as a miracle."

Later, an insurance agent called Ed about the medical forms. "What's a 'spontaneous closure'?" he asked.

Ed smiled. "A miracle."

Brad, now in his thirties, has had no heart problems since God healed him.[2]

The woman forced her way through the crowd. Brad overcame his father's lack of faith. What do you need to push past to get to Jesus?

Like Brad, you might have some naysayers in your life who think you are crazy for believing in the healing power of Jesus.

Maybe what you need God to break through has been the same for so long you struggle to think it could ever change. You have doubts, and you need to push through them. You might be hoping for a relational miracle—your prodigal to come home; your spouse to be willing to work on your marriage; reconciliation with a parent—but it takes two to tango, and you need the other person to cooperate. You might be hoping for a physical miracle, a physical healing. Your need might be financial—or a hundred other things.

You position yourself for a miracle by getting close to Jesus. If there is something you have to push through, push through it.

Realizing Jesus Wants You Close

When the woman who touched Jesus' garment tried to slink away unidentified, Jesus wouldn't have it. He called her to come forward and talk to Him.

Why? She already had her miracle.

I think part of it is that she was moving away from Jesus, and He wanted her close. He wanted to be more than a miracle worker in her life; He wanted a relationship with her. He called her *daughter*.

The same is true for *you*. You need to get close to Jesus to position yourself for a miracle. And what is really amazing is that Jesus wants to be close to you. He is calling you close. He's calling you *son, daughter*.

With Jesus, you are *not* a nobody.

Like the woman we met in the Bible, you might have been told you are.

Like my wife, you might have come to believe you are.

But, no, with Jesus, you are *not* a nobody.

You are a somebody.

You are a somebody who can get close to Jesus. If you get close to Jesus, you are a somebody positioned for a miracle.

CONNECT WITH GOD

Lord, thank You that You have promised to rescue me when I call on You and trust in You. I'm counting on You today. Thank You that You invite me to come close to You. I want to come to You. Help me to risk it all to get near to You. Help me to stay close to You and trust You more. I know Your touch can heal me. I am reaching out for You. I pray in Your name, Jesus, Amen.

POSITION YOURSELF

1. What is a situation in your life that has been bad for so long, it is now easy for you to assume it will always be this way? Talk to God about that. Ask Him to give you faith to know He can still bring change.

2. What would it look like for you to get close to Jesus? What might hold you back or distract you? What practical things could you do today, this week, to get closer to Him? Can you think of any reason why doing those things should not be your most important priority?

3. The woman had to, in faith, reach out and touch Jesus. What might that be for you? What is the final "reach" for you to touch Jesus and receive your miracle?

GROUP DISCUSSION QUESTIONS

1. How close do you feel to Jesus? Why?

2. What are some things you can do right now to get closer to Jesus?

3. What are some things you need to push through that have been keeping you away from Jesus?

4. How does getting close to Jesus change your perspective on situations and challenges in your life?

5. After reading these first three chapters, what is one area that God is challenging you in? What might be your next step?

FOUR

Overcome Fear

There are certain things a person can say to you that immediately induce fear.

"Remember, you have that dentist appointment today." (The dentist strikes fear in my heart.)

"Hi! Looks like I'll be sitting next to you on this five-hour flight. I love to talk!" (A statement that strikes fear in the heart of an introvert.)

"We're out of French fries." (*Noooo!*)

There are also things that cause fear. People struggle with the fear of heights, snakes, public speaking, spiders, clowns. (I will admit clowns are scary.)

But there is one thing that induces fear like nothing else. Your child being sick. Really sick.

Actually, I take that back. There is something worse than your child being sick. Your child being dead.

"Your child is dead" is exactly what happened to Joyce Smith and Antoinette Malombe and the guy in the Bible named Jairus.

Desperate Times Call for . . .

Jairus, as we noted in the last chapter, is a ruler in the synagogue. That is a big deal. The synagogue is the center not only of religion but also of leadership, education and social activity. The synagogue ruler is considered the most important man in town. Jairus has been elevated to this respected position. He has a family, including a daughter he loves. Life is good.

Then life gets a little complicated. A guy named Jesus comes on the scene, traveling from town to town, teaching and, supposedly, doing miracles. This Jesus is radical. He hangs out with sinners. He talks about God's love for everyone. He won't follow manmade rules. The religious leaders are *not* happy and start having meetings to figure out how to get rid of Him. Jairus is a religious leader. He is probably in on those meetings and probably feels the same way.

Then life gets *really* complicated. Jairus's daughter gets sick. At first it seems like no big deal; kids get sick. But Jairus's daughter isn't getting better; she is getting worse. Jairus is confused, then afraid. Her situation becomes increasingly dire.

Jairus is a man of power and wealth. He is able to bring in anyone who might have a cure, but nothing works. His daughter grows worse. She's about to die. Jairus is desperate.

He hears, from his religious colleagues, that Jesus is in town again. They're telling Jairus because they are upset, but Jairus's response is not the same as it has been. This time, instead of thinking, *How do I get Jesus to leave my town?*, Jairus is thinking, *How do I get Jesus to my daughter?*

In Mark 5 we read that powerful Jairus runs to Jesus, falls at His feet and pleads with Him to come save his child.

Desperation is a good thing. I tell people, if you can solve the problem, really there is no problem. And *that's* the problem. Too often we have solutions. America, for instance, is fiercely independent, and we have so much prosperity it can mask our desperation. Your kid is sick? You don't have to run to Jesus, fall at His feet or plead with Him; just drive to Urgent Care.

That's America. That's *not* other parts of the world, like the remote African Congo, where Antoinette Malombe lived. One day, Antoinette heard her two-year-old daughter crying. She ran to the child, Therese, and discovered that she had been bitten by a poisonous snake. Antoinette strapped Therese to her back so she could run for help, but Therese had already stopped breathing.

There was no doctor, no clinic. The only "plan" was Jesus. Antoinette carried her baby on foot over a mountain to get to a Christian friend. When she arrived hours later, all they could do was pray. They must have been tempted to think prayer was futile; Therese had been dead for over three hours. But they overcame fear by letting it be overwhelmed by their faith. They fell at Jesus' feet and cried out to Him for a miracle.

"Your child is dead" is a scary thing, but desperation is a *good* thing.

The Wait

Jesus agrees to go with Jairus, which gives Jairus just a moment of hope. At the same time, he is probably still afraid because he doesn't know if Jesus can get there in time. They have to hurry.

With the throng pressing against them, they make their way toward Jairus's house when . . . a woman who has been bleeding for twelve years somehow pushes her way to Jesus and touches His garment. Jesus stops and announces that someone has touched Him and been healed. The trembling woman comes forward and tells Jesus the whole truth, sharing with Him her whole story.

While . . . Jairus is watching and waiting. He is dying inside. Jesus just healed some woman who's been sick for a long time, but his daughter is about to die. Now Jesus has stopped *to talk to* this woman, who has *already* been healed—while his daughter is at the edge of death. It makes no sense. Can you imagine a doctor, who has the power to heal, asking a woman in a hallway, who is now fine, to tell him her story while a little girl is dying in the emergency room? He would be sued for malpractice.

Jairus must be desperate and afraid, thinking, *What are You doing, Jesus? Don't You understand my situation? Don't You care? Why won't You hurry?*

Do you ever feel that way? You need help *now*, but God doesn't seem to hear your cries for help. You look around and other people are enjoying life with God, and He is paying attention to them and answering their prayers, but He seems to be ignoring you.

How do you feel in that moment? Do you find yourself overwhelmed with fear?

Don't Be Afraid

Jesus is having a conversation with a woman who no longer needs to be healed, when the thing Jairus fears most happens. Some people from his house arrive with a message: "Your daughter is dead."

Can you imagine how Jairus feels? Not only is his heart broken, but he is probably full of anger for Jesus, who refused to hurry.

In that moment, Jesus looks at him calmly. "Ignoring what they said, Jesus told the synagogue ruler, 'Don't be afraid; just believe'" (Mark 5:36 NIV 1984).

Jesus *ignores* what they said. If you want to position yourself for a miracle you *have to* overcome fear, and to overcome fear you *have to* ignore what they say. Who are *they*? *They* are the doctors who tell you there is no hope. *They* are your friends who invite you to the bar even though they know you want to stop drinking. *They* are the parents who say you'll never change. *They* are the people at church who tell you God doesn't do miracles anymore. You *have to* ignore what they say.

Jesus ignores what they said. Then He tells Jairus, "Don't be afraid; just believe."

Don't be afraid? It might sound impossible, but the truth is that Jairus has a choice: fear or faith? Believe it's over *or* believe in the healing power of Jesus. It is a crucial choice. Fear will *hold back* the healing power of Jesus; faith will *release* the healing power of Jesus.

When we face bad situations we have the same choice: fear or faith?

It's easy to buy into fear when we face impossibilities. Our minds always take us to worst-case scenarios. We get wrapped up in the "What if?" questions. *What if the chemo doesn't work? What if God won't help me? What if I lose my house? What if I can never kick this habit . . . forgive my dad . . . find someone to marry?*

It's easy to give in to fear, but we need to choose faith. We can't have both. Some people say they have faith, but they are also afraid. I don't think fear and faith can coexist. We choose *one*. Will we be overwhelmed by fear, or will we overcome fear with faith?

I challenge people, when they are afraid, to ask God this question: *What is at the root of my fear?* It may seem obvious: "The scary circumstances I'm facing are the root of my fear!" I urge you to look deeper. If you really believe in a God who is bigger than your circumstances, your circumstances shouldn't scare you. So, what is truly at the root of your fear?

I often find, for instance, that people's fear stems from being disappointed with God in the past. Something bad happened; they blamed God; and now they feel as though they can't trust Him.

The problem with that thinking is that whatever bad thing happened *wasn't* from God. God loves us and gives us good and perfect gifts (see James 1:17). Jesus came so He could give us full, abundant life (see John 10:10). So why do bad things happen? Not because of God, but because we have an enemy who targets us to steal from, and to kill and destroy (see John 10:10). Sometimes bad things happen because we make bad decisions, and we suffer the consequences. Bad things also happen because other people make bad decisions, and we suffer because of their sin.

Whatever happened, it *wasn't* God. But your enemy will try to get you to think it was. From the beginning he has been whispering in people's ears, "God's not good. He's holding out on you. He's to blame."

No, that's a lie. If you buy into that lie you will be afraid when crisis hits because you will think, *God's doing it to me again.* No. God didn't do it to you last time. God loves you. He is a good Father and He is trustworthy.

I encourage people, when they are afraid, to determine the root of their fear *and* to take each fearful thought and turn it over to God. Make a choice that you will not entertain *one single* fearful thought. The battle is being waged in our thought lives. One fearful thought can become contagious. The Bible says, "We demolish arguments and every pretension that sets itself up against the knowledge of God, and we take captive every thought to make it obedient to Christ" (2 Corinthians 10:5). Fearful thoughts *will* come at you, but consider each one a cancer, and get rid of it, *immediately*. Grab it and make it subservient to God's truth. Take every fearful thought, see that it's a lie designed to trip you up, give it to God and ask Him, "What's Your truth? What do You want to give me to replace the fear?"

Then listen.

What is God saying to you? What is He giving you to replace the fear? You may hear God saying, *I want to give you My peace.* Or

I will bring good out of this. Or *You are more than a conqueror through Jesus who loves you.* Or *I love you. You can trust Me.* Or you may hear God saying what He said to Jairus: *Don't be afraid; just believe.*

Keep Moving

It's the moment of truth for Jairus. Jesus tells him, "Don't be afraid; just believe." Will Jairus choose fear or faith?

Jairus chooses . . . faith. That is so encouraging to me. If Jairus can overcome fear with faith when he is told his daughter is dead, you and I can make that same decision.

If Jairus had chosen fear, he would have given up and left Jesus behind. Because he chose faith, he and Jesus keep moving. They continue walking through the crowd on their rescue mission to heal Jairus's once sick, but now dead, daughter.

That journey reminds me of Antoinette. She picked up her dead daughter to go to a faith-filled friend who could help her ask Jesus for healing. She must have been tempted to give up. Maybe even to jettison her faith; after all, wasn't God to blame for what just happened? But she took those fearful thoughts captive, recognized them as lies and chose faith. She kept moving.

What would it look like for *you* to keep moving to the place where God can break through?

Send Them Out

Jesus and Jairus arrive at the house where they find a big crowd of people "crying and wailing loudly." Jesus says, "Why all this commotion and wailing? The child is not dead but asleep" (Mark 5:38–39). Everyone laughs at Him. You can't really blame them. They know a dead child when they see one, and the girl is dead.

I love the next line: "After he put them all out . . ." Jesus *throws them out.* In the original language, the verb translated "put them all out" is the exact same word used to describe what Jesus did to the moneychangers in the Temple. It's the same verb used 38 times to describe what Jesus did to demons. Jesus did not politely ask demons to leave. He didn't request delicately that the moneychangers step outside. Jesus *ordered* the demons; He *violently threw out* the moneychangers; and here He *forcefully* makes all the mourners leave.

When John Smith was in the ICU at Cardinal Glennon, first dead, and then barely hanging on to life, Joyce and I "put out" of the room anyone who expressed doubts. Why? We were following the example of Jesus and, I think, did it for the same reason as Jesus. To position ourselves for a miracle we need to overcome fear and choose faith. Anyone who was doing the opposite, who was choosing fear and ignoring faith, was a distraction if not a straight-out deterrent.

I wonder if there is anyone you need to "put out of the room" right now. I know it's difficult—it wasn't easy for us to act like bouncers in the ICU—but it is necessary.

Expect a Resurrection

Jesus takes Jairus and his wife into the room where their daughter is lying dead. He takes the child's hand and says, *"Talitha koum!"* ("Little girl, get up!") Jairus's dead daughter does as she is told. The dead girl wakes up, stands up and starts walking around as if nothing had happened.

We are told that "they were completely astonished." Yeah, they were astonished. They were hoping Jesus could cure sickness; they weren't looking for Him to resurrect the dead. People may believe a healing is possible, but no one expects a resurrection.

No one expects a resurrection . . . except God. He sees resurrections coming. That's why Jesus told Jairus, "Don't be afraid; just believe."

No one expects a resurrection except God *and* people who know Him and believe.

I *love* the prayer Paul prays in Ephesians 1. He starts out, "I pray for you constantly, asking God . . . to give you spiritual wisdom and insight so that you might grow in your knowledge of God" (verses 16–17 NLT). The prayer is that we might grow in *truly* knowing God. Why? We need to know we have a God who loves us and is a good, trustworthy Father.

The prayer continues: "I also pray that you will understand the incredible greatness of God's power for us who believe him. This is the same mighty power that raised Christ from the dead" (verses 19–20 NLT).

Read that again.

Read it one more time.

This is saying that the *same power* that God used to raise Jesus from the dead is available to you. It is incredibly great power, and you can have it at work in *your* life.

Who sees a resurrection coming? People who believe those words. People who know God and know He has resurrection power and know He has given that same power to us.

Like Joyce Smith. She walked into the emergency room to discover that her son had been dead for over an hour. What was her response? *Don't be afraid; just believe.* She chose faith over fear. Fearful thoughts shot at her, of course, but she grabbed them, took them captive, rejected them and chose instead to believe in the incredible greatness of God's power that raised Christ from the dead. She overcame fear—and not only did her son come back to life; he suffered no ill effects. Soon he was back in school and on the basketball court.

Who sees a resurrection coming? Antoinette did. Rather than give in to fear, she carried her dead daughter over a mountain. *Don't be afraid; just believe.* She and her friend cried out to Jesus together. They overcame fear—and Therese began breathing.

Not only was she alive, but she suffered no brain damage. She grew up, went to seminary and entered into full-time ministry.[1]

One thing induces fear like nothing else: Your child being dead. Really dead. It happened to Joyce Smith and Antoinette Malombe and Jairus.

And it happened to someone else. Do you know who?

God.

God knows what it's like to watch your child die. He knows that pain.

But God saw the resurrection coming.

He has resurrection power.

He can raise a dead child, a dead marriage, a dead career, dead finances, a dead relationship.

He has resurrection power, and, because He loves us, He has made that incredibly great power available to us.

We position ourselves for a miracle by overcoming fear with faith.

CONNECT WITH GOD

Father, when life comes at me, I'm tempted to be afraid. Sometimes it feels as though all I can see is the problem. But, from this day forward, I choose faith. What I will see is You—and Your power. When fearful thoughts come at me, I will take them captive and make them obedient to Christ. God, I want to replace fear with Your peace. I know that You are a good Father who gives good gifts to Your children. I know You sent Jesus so I can have abundant life in You. I know that, in Christ, I am more than a conqueror. Please help me not to be afraid and just to believe. Amen.

POSITION YOURSELF

1. Decide what is going to rule your life: faith or fear. What you choose will determine much of what God is able to do in your life. Whenever fear starts to creep in, stop and pray. Take the thought captive. Hold it up to the truth and see it for the lie it is. Ask God what He wants to give you to replace the lie.

2. If you have felt let down by God in the past, take a few minutes to share your heart with Him. Talk to Him about every disappointment, and then ask Him to reveal His truth to you. Listen quietly and wait patiently for His answer.

3. Is there anyone or anything you need to "put out" of your life right now, because it's a distraction or a deterrent to your overcoming fear and having the faith you need to position yourself for a miracle? When will you do what you need to do?

GROUP DISCUSSION QUESTIONS

1. What is your greatest fear? Why?

2. What is a verse (or two!) in the Bible where God talks about fear? Would you commit to memorizing a verse (or two!) to help you combat fear?

3. When you are afraid, what is your "go to" position? Where does your mind immediately turn? What do you find yourself wanting to do?

4. How could you make God your "go to" when you feel afraid?

5. The enemy uses lies to build fear in our lives. What lies might you be believing? What is God's truth about those lies?

6. What would be a good strategy to help you choose faith over fear?

FIVE

Live Desperate

There is a book called *The Worst-Case Scenario Survival Handbook*.[1] Each chapter gives you simple steps to handle life's most desperate moments.

One chapter is "How to Escape from Quicksand." Another teaches "How to Win a Sword Fight." Umm. Thanks, but, well, not really sure I'll run into either of those situations.

Another chapter covers "How to Escape from a Mountain Lion." The first step is, "Do not run." That sounds easy. I am almost always not running. But I am guessing that when you encounter a mountain lion, not running is not easy. The main strategy for escaping from a mountain lion is to try to intimidate it by making yourself appear larger than you are. How? "If you have small children with you, pick them up—do all you can to appear larger." They don't tell you how to convince the child to go along with this plan. They also don't estimate how much you will end up paying for therapy sessions, as your kid deals with the psychological damage you inflicted by using them as a human shield.

The book seeks to give easy-to-follow steps for life's most desperate situations. We all know it is *not* that easy. When the doctor says "cancer," when you are staring at bankruptcy, when you can't stop hating yourself for what you did, when your kids' medical bills are more than you can afford, when your spouse starts talking about divorce, it is *never* easy and simple strategies *do not* work.

When we face worst-case scenarios, when storms hit our lives, we feel desperate. We don't like that feeling, so we try to avoid it. We ignore the situation or pretend things are not that bad. We miss the fact that God has a gift for us in our desperation. The gift is God. Pastor Kyle Idleman, in his book *Don't Give Up*, writes, "We avoid desperation, simply hoping the situation takes it upon itself to clear up; waiting for the darkness to lighten up. But what if the desperation is a grace disguised?"[2]

When we are desperate we have an opportunity to cry out to God, and to experience His presence and power in a way we maybe never have before. We want that. We want deliverance. We just don't want to be desperate to get it. But the place we find God and experience His miracles is often in the middle of the storm.

The Storm Hits

One evening Jesus tells His disciples He wants to cross the lake with them.

As they are making their way to the other side, a storm comes up. This is no surprise because this "lake" is the Sea of Galilee, which is notorious for ferocious, unpredictable storms. It is located about six hundred feet below sea level and is virtually surrounded by mountains. The topography acts like a giant funnel drawing cold air down from those mountains and blasting it onto the sea. That frigid air hitting the water can stir up instant and violent storms. In fact, it is typical in the midst of a big storm for waves to reach a height of twenty feet.

Jesus' friends, the disciples, start freaking out when this storm hits. What is interesting is that several of them are experienced sailors. They have been through all kinds of storms, but apparently this one goes beyond their ability, and they are desperate.

My friend Brian knows what it is like to feel desperate and unable to fix a situation. At the church I pastored in Port Angeles, Washington, we had prayed that God would help us reach addicts who were far from Him. Brian was an answer to that prayer. He was struggling with drug addiction, and he started showing up at our church.

When we are desperate, we have an opportunity to cry out to God, and that is exactly what Brian did at home one Friday night. He prayed a desperate prayer: "God, if You are real, I need You. I want to know You are real." Suddenly, and I am not making this up, a storm broke. Brian heard thunder outside. He looked out his window and saw lightning illuminating the sky. Oddly, though, the lightning was blazing horizontally. And, perhaps more unusual, there was no rain. Thunder and lightning, but no rain, and it lasted for 48 straight hours. Brian came to church on Sunday and gave his life to Jesus.

Not long later, another storm hit Brian's life. One morning his son, Aayden, complained of not feeling good. Brian took his temperature—it was 104.3. He took Aayden to the hospital, where the doctors told him they had a sense it might be bacterial spinal meningitis.

The next day I got a call from Brian. His son was about to be airlifted to Children's Hospital in Seattle. I jumped into my car and was able to get there in time to pray over Aayden before they put him in the helicopter. When he got to the hospital, tests showed bacteria in his spinal fluid and blood. The doctors were very concerned. Brian was desperate.

You know what it's like. You have had storms overtake your life as well. You get word that you have lost your job, or you read a text you weren't supposed to read, or you get a call like the one Joyce got about John. It's amazing to me how fast life can turn upside down. When the storm hits, desperation hits, and you don't know what to do.

Where Is God in the Storm?

The storm on the Sea of Galilee rages, and it seems as though the disciples immediately start trying to save themselves. They think, *We have this,* but it quickly becomes obvious they *don't* have this.

What you do when a storm comes says a lot about you. Think: When a storm hits your life, what is your "go to" position? What is your immediate response? Do you try to fix it yourself? How long does it take to admit you don't have this?

The disciples realize they are in trouble, and they freak out.

Little do they know . . . this desperate situation is covered in *The Worst-Case Scenario Survival Handbook*! What should they do? "Get in the life raft, and take whatever supplies you can carry."[3] Well, I'm pretty sure the disciples didn't have a life raft. So the book gives another simple step: "If you see a plane . . . nearby, try to signal."[4] No, there would be no planes coming to their rescue.

Okay, the handbook wouldn't help them. But there is something else they don't seem to know: Desperate situations are covered *by Jesus*. They are losing it because of the storm, but in the boat with them is the ruler of storms. Finally, they have that epiphany, so they turn to Jesus and . . . He is sleeping.

I never know what to make of that. The Perfect Storm is about to flood and capsize their boat, and Jesus is snoozing. Apparently, Jesus is (1) a heavy sleeper, and (2) not freaked out by storms.

The disciples seem confused that Jesus is sleeping. Jesus' disciples *today* can be confused when storms hit, and they pray, and nothing happens, and it seems as if Jesus is sleeping.

That is what happened with Brian. He assumed that when we prayed for Aayden, God would immediately make him better. But Aayden did not get better. He got worse. Was Jesus not paying attention? Was He asleep? The storm intensified, Brian became more desperate, and it felt bad, but *it was a good thing*.

When *we* have the sense that God is not paying attention, that He might even be sleeping when He is supposed to be on watch, we become *more* desperate, and that feels bad, but *it is a good thing*. The problem is that too often we are *not* desperate. We need to *live desperate* and, when we do, we are positioning ourselves for a miracle.

Look what happened on the Sea of Galilee.

Jesus was in the stern, sleeping on a cushion. The disciples woke him and said to him, "Teacher, don't you care if we drown?"

He got up, rebuked the wind and said to the waves, "Quiet! Be still!" Then the wind died down and it was completely calm.

He said to his disciples, "Why are you so afraid? Do you still have no faith?"

They were terrified and asked each other, "Who is this? Even the wind and the waves obey him!"

Mark 4:38–41

God made a promise to you a long time ago. It is a promise you need to be aware of, maybe even know by heart. David wrote it: "The Lord hears his people when they call to him for help. He rescues them from all their troubles. The Lord is close to the brokenhearted; he rescues those whose spirits are crushed" (Psalm 34:17–18 NLT).

God is close to the brokenhearted. He rescues us when we cry out to Him for help. The issue is that too often we ignore our brokenness and refuse to ask for help. That is why desperation is so vital. It forces us to pray desperate prayers. Just before sharing that promise from God, David confided, "In my desperation I prayed" (Psalm 34:6 NLT).

Often, it's not until we realize we are desperate—until we are willing to *admit* that we are desperate—that we finally cry out to God. When we let out that desperate cry, we are positioning ourselves to experience a miracle, and to experience God in a way we never have before.

That is what happens with the disciples. They cry out, Jesus calms the storm, and they have a profoundly new understanding of who Jesus is and what He is capable of.

That is also what happened with Brian.

Brian called from Children's Hospital, telling us the tests revealed bacteria in Aayden's spinal fluid and blood. Prayer requests immediately went out through our church and on Facebook.

The doctors took another sample of Aayden's blood the next day and found even *more* signs of bacterial meningitis. The storm was still raging, and all Brian could do was call out to Jesus. Joining him were hundreds, maybe thousands, of people all crying out desperate prayers.

The next day the doctors took another sample of Aayden's blood, and they found *no sign* of the infection. The doctors were confused and amazed. Brian says it was as if God reached down and pulled the bacteria out of Aayden's blood. Here is what he wrote on Facebook:[5]

Let me express how grateful we are for your prayers, and how serious the power of prayer can be. Tuesday we were flown to Seattle for my son's spinal meningitis. It was serious. Yesterday we were told that thanks to Port Angeles hospital's quickness his life had been saved. I also believe, however, that the hundreds of prayers, texts and calls played a huge role in the news I'm about to tell. It was confirmed he had bacteria growing in his blood and spine—and the most dangerous sort. But this afternoon the docs came in with yesterday's blood work—and the bacteria is completely gone. As if God just reached in and removed it. Wow! So truly amazing. We still have to stay another week here, but it's a week to think how precious life is and how special prayer and God are. I will never be able to express my gratitude to the fullest, but my life from here forward will prove it. Thank you to all who took the time to love us. I owe you my son's life!

I will say it again: When we are desperate we have an opportunity to cry out to God, and to experience His presence and power in a way we maybe never have before. We want that. We want deliverance. We just never want to be desperate to get it. But the place we find God and experience His miracles is often in the middle of the storm.

Storms can come out of nowhere. I think of the time I was leading a children's ministry, and we were promoting Sidewalk Sunday School. We were trying to get kids to come, so an hour before it started, we were out offering candy to kids in the neighborhood.

A four-year-old saw us and started to run across the street to us. I watched the car coming. It felt like watching slow motion, but, in reality, it was happening so fast I could do nothing. The car slammed into the child at full speed. He flipped over the car, ended up underneath it, and somehow got hooked up so it dragged him until the car screeched to a stop.

I was sure he had to be dead. I felt completely desperate. I cried out to God. I prayed to God for breakthrough, for the child to be alive, for him somehow to have no serious injuries. We ran over and found him . . . alive. He had no serious injuries. The only evidence of the impact was a small burn he had from the muffler.

Are you in the middle of a storm? Is it making you feel desperate, and pushing you to focus on Jesus and cry out to Him?

Or I wonder if there is something in your life that isn't good, but you have been tolerating it because it is easier just to pretend everything is fine than to have to admit you don't have this, and feel that desperation.

It could be that your teenager has been drifting away from God, and you are increasingly seeing signs that there are pockets of secret sin. But you don't want to think that. That is too scary to acknowledge. So, rather than feeling desperate and really crying out to Jesus, you pretend it is not happening and let your kid continue to slide.

Maybe you have an addiction that you would never call an addiction. It might be that what you are doing too much of doesn't seem *that* bad—shopping, eating. Or you know that you are just doing what lots of people are doing—pornography. You should be desperate, you should be crying out to Jesus, but, instead, you just keep living a "less than" life instead of experiencing the overcoming life God has for you.

Perhaps your marriage is not what you hoped it would be. It's not horrible, but it's not good. Still, no one has mentioned it and you are afraid to. The conversation could lead to chaos. Rather than feeling desperate and really crying out to Jesus, you have decided it is easier just to continue pretending things are good.

If you would be willing to admit you are desperate, you would be positioning yourself for a miracle, and your life could really change.

God can do something amazing if you just live desperate and cry out to Him.

Cry Out

One day my phone rang. It was Jennifer, a friend of ours, and I could tell from her voice that she was panicking.

"Jason, the doctors say my mother has fifteen minutes to live. She's not going to make it, and she doesn't know the Lord." Jennifer's mom had been sick for a while, but I think when *fifteen minutes* came out of the doctor's mouth, a new level of desperation set in.

I told her I would come. When I walked into the hospital room, Jennifer looked at me with big scared eyes, then looked at her mom. I followed her gaze. I didn't know if her mom was in a coma or sleeping or in the middle of dying, but her eyes were closed and it was clear she was oblivious to what was happening in the room.

I walked over to her, leaned in and whispered in her ear: "You are standing on the edge of eternity. This is your last chance. Jesus loves you, and it's your time. You've got to make that decision. If you want to accept Jesus into your life right now, squeeze my hand."

I felt a faint squeeze.

I was about to tell Jennifer what had happened, but when I turned around to face her, I saw two angels in the room. I had never seen anything like that.

I stood there, stunned, for a moment. Then I told Jennifer that her mom had squeezed my hand. When we looked back at her mom, we could have sworn her toes were going from gray to pink. Then there was color in her ankles, and then her knees started to change.

Within fifteen minutes she opened her eyes and exclaimed, "I gave my heart to Jesus!"

An hour later, all of her vitals were back to normal. The nurses came in and could not believe it.

The next day she was well enough to go home.

There is no chapter in *The Worst-Case Scenario Survival Handbook* to consult for "What to do when your mother is given fifteen minutes to live, and she doesn't believe in Jesus." There are no easy-to-follow simple steps. No, the only answer is desperation.

This daughter had been concerned about her mom in the past, but when she finally became truly desperate, she called out to Jesus. And in her desperation she experienced God's presence and power in a way she never had before.

The mother had heard about Jesus in the past, but when she finally became truly desperate, she called out to Him. And in her desperation she experienced God's presence and power in a way she never had before.

No one likes to feel desperate. We may even try to avoid it. But God has a gift for us in our desperation. Live desperate and cry out to Him.

CONNECT WITH GOD

God, I don't like it when storms hit my life. I don't like chaos or being out of control. I don't like feeling desperate, and maybe I try to avoid it. But I realize that when I am desperate, I am more likely to turn to You and to cry out to You. And when I am desperate, I realize that You are in control, and that You are close, and that You will rescue me. So, God, help me to "live desperate," to have a constant awareness that I really need You. Because God, I do really need You. In Jesus' name, Amen.

POSITION YOURSELF

1. What area of your life has felt desperate lately? Have you truly called out to Jesus? What exactly might it look like for you to do that? How do you think you might experience God in the midst of that storm?

2. In what area of your life have you been ignoring desperation for a long time? Is there something that isn't right, but you act as though it is? What will it take for you to admit it is desperate and call out to Jesus?

3. Commit to memorizing Psalm 34:17–18 (NLT): "The LORD hears his people when they call to him for help. He rescues them from all their troubles. The LORD is close to the brokenhearted; he rescues those whose spirits are crushed."

GROUP DISCUSSION QUESTIONS

1. When was a time your life was hit by an unexpected storm? What impact did it have on you?

2. What do you tend to do when a storm comes into your life?

3. How can you prepare for future storms that will come into your life?

4. Do you think it would help to write down some of the promises God has made to you in the Bible? If so, will you do it?

5. Those promises God has given: Have you given up on them, or are you pressing in and holding on to them?

6. How do we live a life that is desperate for God in the good times and the bad?

SIX

Believe Big, Pray Big

Richard Harvey was a medical missionary, a doctor who goes to another country and offers free medical help as a part of a Christian missionary effort. In his book *70 Years of Miracles,* he tells an amazing story. While Harvey was a student at Allegheny College in Meadville, Pennsylvania, a chemistry professor, Dr. Lee, would give a certain lecture every year just before Thanksgiving break. It became known as the prayer lecture.[1]

Dr. Lee would stand before his students and say something like this: "Well, ladies and gentlemen, here we are, the last class before everyone goes home for Thanksgiving. Now, Thanksgiving is a holiday in which a lot of people consume vast amounts of food, and before they do this, they give thanks to this being they call the Creator. And many of them will have special services in their churches. And they will do this thing called praying. Is there anyone here who still believes in this thing called prayer? Because if there is, I have an experiment that I would like to conduct today."

At that juncture Dr. Lee would hold up a flask. Then, his sarcasm evident, he would make a challenge: He would propose dropping the flask. Any student who believed in prayer was invited to pray that the fragile glass would not shatter as it hit the floor.

Harvey said that he himself was too intimidated to accept the challenge—as were the other students. For some fifteen years Dr. Lee made his irreverent remarks without a taker.

Then one afternoon early in Harvey's senior year, he heard a knock at his door. It was a freshman who asked point-blank if he was a Christian. When Harvey said yes, the freshman went on to explain that he had heard about Dr. Lee's prayer lecture and wanted to have the courage to stand up to the professor and pray that the flask not break. He was asking the Christians on campus to pray for him.

Harvey agreed but admitted that he was worried for the young man.

Finally, the day came for Dr. Lee's prayer lecture right before Thanksgiving break. Harvey skipped a class in order to be there to see what would happen. So did many other students; the room was packed.

Dr. Lee rose to his feet and started his speech. "Well, ladies and gentlemen," he began, and concluded with the familiar words, "Is there anyone in this lecture hall who still believes in prayer?"

I want to stop the story because I need to ask you: What would you do in that situation? If you were in that class, in that lecture hall, what would you do?

I think the answer to that question says a lot about whether or not you believe in a big God, and in the power of big prayers.

The reality is *if* you believe in a big God, you will pray big prayers and see big miracles. But many of us don't. I want to share a story with you where Jesus' disciples were not believing big.

If You Can

In Mark 9:14–29 we read that Jesus and a few of His disciples are coming down from a mountain and find the other disciples arguing with a man. Jesus asks what they are arguing about, and the man explains that he has a mute son who is possessed buy a spirit and needs healing. The disciples had tried to heal him, but were unsuccessful.

Jesus' response is, "You unbelieving generation."

What is the problem? The disciples don't believe—or at least don't believe *big*.

Later, the disciples pull Jesus aside and ask why they couldn't heal the boy, and Jesus explains, "This kind can come out only by prayer."

Wait. Hold up. The disciples tried to heal the kid . . . *without praying?* So they don't believe big *and* they don't pray big.

The father complains that the disciples were no help to his son, and then he says to Jesus, "But if you can do anything, take pity on us and help us."

Jesus responds, "'If you can'? . . . Everything is possible for one who believes."

Then comes a moment of questionable faith but great honesty. "Immediately the boy's father exclaimed, 'I do believe; help me overcome my unbelief!'"

The disciples are not believing big and, apparently, are not praying at all. The father might actually have more faith than they have, but he definitely has doubts mixed in. No wonder the miracle didn't happen before Jesus showed up!

But the miracle *does* happen now. Jesus turns from the dad's mixture of faith and doubt and heals his son. That encourages me. I love seeing that when this father is honest with Jesus about his doubts, Jesus has grace on him. And I bet what happened moves the dad to bigger belief.

Jesus wants to move us to bigger belief. We need to believe big and pray big.

Believe Bigger

Sometimes people will say to me, "I just need to have more faith." No, you don't. People ask, "How do I grow my faith?" You don't.

Jesus' disciples asked Him once, "Show us how to increase our faith."

Jesus told them, "If you had faith even as small as a mustard seed, you could say to this mulberry tree, 'May you be uprooted and thrown into the sea,' and it would obey you!" (Luke 17:5–6 NLT).

We have faith or we don't.

The issue is this: Do we *believe*?

I think of it this way: *Faith* is believing there is a God. *Belief* is believing that God will do what He says He will do. That is why we don't see Jesus asking people to have faith, or if they have faith. But He asked people *repeatedly*, "Do you believe I can do this?"

Faith gets you into heaven, but it is belief that positions you for a miracle.

We need to grow our belief, so we can believe big.

How do you grow your belief?

Part of it is getting into God's Word. You need to know God, and know God's promises, and know the stories of when God was faithful to His promises. When you do, you will realize that God *can*, and you will believe that God *will*. You will overcome the "if you can" mentality and move into a firm "everything is possible for one who believes" mindset.

Another part of growing your belief is actually believing God for things. Belief is how we put our faith into action. We could say that faith is kind of like *having* muscles, and belief is like *using* your muscles. What grows our muscles is going to the gym and using them. (Though I wouldn't actually know this personally!) What grows our belief is *using* it. When we actively believe God can and God will, we see God work, and our belief grows. What we are doing is positioning ourselves for a miracle because big belief leads to big prayers, and big prayers lead to big miracles.

Pray Bigger

When we believe big, we pray big.

I think too often we pray timid prayers because we are afraid: What if God doesn't answer? That reveals an "if you can" lack of belief.

One thing to remember: We don't control the outcome. We pray for the outcome we seek, but we don't control it. We need to trust God with the outcome. Trusting God with the outcome gives us boldness. If He chooses to give what we ask for, that is awesome. If He chooses not to give us the outcome we request, we trust Him all the same.

We believe big, and we pray big.

Maybe you are not quite there yet. Good news: You can get there. You can learn this.

Just like that dad who had belief *and* unbelief, but then had his unbelief trumped by seeing Jesus do the impossible, you can grow your belief and learn how to pray big.

Just like Shara.

Shara was a local business owner who started attending our church in Port Angeles. She knew about Jesus, but I am not sure how much she really *knew* Jesus. She had attended church before, but a lot of what we talked about seemed new to her.

One day Shara called me in a panic. "Jason, Dave is on the floor. I called 911, but I don't know what to do. We need you here!"

It turns out that Dave, Shara's husband, had been spraying insecticide into their trees in the yard and had inhaled a lot of it. Dave had had asthma in the past, and inhaling the bug spray immediately started to petrify his lungs. He stumbled into the kitchen, grabbed onto a cabinet and fell to the floor. He couldn't breathe.

My wife and I arrived just after the paramedics. Dave had been lying on the floor for ten minutes. The paramedics were trying to do CPR but were not successful because Dave's lungs had become so petrified his chest was as hard as a wood table. From the faces and comments of the paramedics I realized they thought Dave was not going to make it.

Shara looked distraught. Paula and I began praying, believing God was going to show His power. The paramedics tried to give Dave a shot in his chest with a huge needle, but apparently his chest was simply too hard. They rushed him to the ambulance and to the hospital. Paula and I followed in our car.

I walked into the emergency room as Shara asked the doctor, "Can you give me some hope?"

He said, "Sorry. Today, I can give you no hope."

I wasn't having it. I shouted, "Anyone who's not a believer, leave the room!"

No one left. (I'm not sure if they were believers in Jesus, or if they were just believers in my not having authority over their emergency room.)

I walked over to Dave and saw that blood was coming out of his nose and ears. I laid my hands on him and prayed big: "God, You are the master creator and physician. Put Dave back together better than before. Fill his lungs with oxygen. Let him have no brain damage."

The doctor said that Dave had no heart or brain activity and talked about taking him off life support. I kept praying. The doctor left. I kept praying. The doctor came back in—and was shocked to see Dave breathing.

Soon they moved Dave out of the ER, but still the doctor wasn't offering Shara any hope.

"Honestly," the doctor said, "even if he lives. His brain . . . isn't going to function. He's . . . he's not going to be the same. It will be bad."

I kept believing big and praying big. "God, let Shara and Dave be surrounded by angels. God, put Dave back together better than before."

Soon the doctors decided to take Dave off life support. When they did, Dave's eyes opened. Literally. At that moment.

Dave was supposed to die, but instead he recovered, immediately. The next day he was out of the hospital.

I asked Shara recently about all that had happened.

She said, "That's when I learned to pray big."

God is still in the miracle business. If you need a miracle, you believe big and you learn to pray big.

What if Lots Believed Big and Prayed Big?

If you *really* want to position yourself for a miracle, believe big, pray big, *and get a bunch of other people believing big and praying big on your behalf.* Jesus tells us there is extra power when extra people are praying (see Matthew 18:20). Amazing things happen; things that could *never* happen *happen* when lots of people petition God for a miracle.

As a teenager, Barbara was diagnosed with progressive multiple sclerosis at the Mayo Clinic. Her condition worsened; she spent months in hospitals, her diaphragm became paralyzed, a lung became nonfunctional, her other lung operated at less than fifty percent. A tracheostomy tube was inserted in her neck; she could only talk by putting something in the hole before she began to speak. She was unable to breathe on her own, requiring continuous oxygen. A catheter was inserted into her bladder and a colostomy bag attached to collect her bodily waste. She went legally blind, and a feeding tube was inserted in her stomach.

One of her physicians, Dr. Harold P. Adolph, said, "Barbara was one of the most hopelessly ill patients I ever saw."

In 1981, Barbara entered hospice care. She had not been able to walk for seven years and had a life expectancy of fewer than six months.

One day someone called the radio station of the Moody Bible Institute in Chicago and shared Barbara's story, asking people to pray. Who knows how many people prayed, but more than 450 letters were sent to her church by Christians who promised they were praying for her.

Barbara's aunt and a few friends went to her and read some of the letters. Suddenly Barbara heard a man's voice saying, *My child, get up and walk.*

She *did.* She took out her oxygen tube, stood up, started walking *and* could see again. That night she went to church!

The next day she went to see one of her doctors. Stunned, he examined her, then finally said, "This is medically impossible. But you are now free to go out and live your life."

Two of Barbara's doctors were so amazed by what happened they published the story.[2]

Dr. Adolph attests that "she was eventually restored to complete health."

Barbara has now lived, completely healthy, for more than 35 years.

Another of her doctors, Dr. Thomas Marshall, wrote, "I have never witnessed anything like this before or since and considered it a rare privilege to observe the hand of God performing a true miracle."

What led to the miracle? Believing big and praying big. *Lots of people believing big and praying big prayers.*

Speaking of big prayers, that brings us back to Dr. Lee's prayer challenge. . . .

Does Anybody Here Still Believe in Prayer?

Dr. Lee was giving his famous prayer lecture and finally reached the part where he asked, "Is there anybody here who still believes in prayer?"

The faith-filled freshman was sitting in the middle of the room. He raised his hand and answered, "Yes, Dr. Lee. I do."

Dr. Lee asked the young man to stand. Then he explained the experiment, making sure the freshman understood it clearly. Satisfied that he did, Dr. Led invited the student to pray.

Harvey says that the prayer was simple. The student asked God, for His name's sake and for His glory, to keep the flask from breaking.

Then, with an amused smile, Dr. Lee held the flask between two fingers and let go.

With every eye glued to the descent, the glass dropped. It landed on the toe of Dr. Lee's shoe and rolled onto the floor, without breaking.

The class went nuts. Dr. Lee demanded that everyone leave the room, and he never gave the prayer lecture again.

Harvey writes that he went back to his room, fell on his knees and cried. He had sat through that lecture, as had many other Christians, without saying a word. His final thoughts were, *Help me, God, to live as if I believe in You!*

Wouldn't it be great if we lived as if we believed in God? What might happen if we believed big and prayed big? I don't know all that might go down, but I do know that we would be positioning ourselves for some big miracles.

CONNECT WITH GOD

God, I want to know You more. The more I know You, the more I'll believe. I want to have bigger faith; please give me that. Help me overcome my unbelief. Father, I know that because You are powerful, prayers to You are powerful. Help me not only to believe big but to pray big. I know that sometimes it will require risk, so help me to take big risks. I want to live a big life with You and see big miracles. Thank You for Your big love for me. I pray in Jesus' name, Amen.

POSITION YOURSELF

1. You need a *pro*active prayer life, not a *re*active prayer life. Prayer is not just for emergencies. Prayer is at the heart of our connection with God. We need to have a consistent prayer time every day, and we need to pray consistently throughout the rest of the day. How is your connection with God? What changes could you make to prioritize having a focused prayer time with God each day, and to help you continue to focus on God throughout the day?

2. Pray specific prayers. Don't just pray for a miracle: If you need a healing, pray for a healing. And don't just pray for a healing, pray specifically for the damaged lungs, or for God to remove the brain tumor, or for the kidney to start functioning again. You don't have to tell God *how* to do it. You can trust Him to figure that out. He may heal mysteriously or through the skills of a doctor or through medication. Pray for specific outcomes, and leave the details of *how* to God.

3. Keep praying. I tell people to *PUSH*—Pray Until Something Happens. It's not "one and done." Keep going to God. Not because God needs us to go to Him over and over, but because we need to pray over and over. Each time you pray, you are lining up your heart with God's heart. Keep praying. Persistent prayers are powerful.

4. Start praising. Don't spend so much time praying about your problem that you forget to praise Him for His answer. No matter what is happening, God deserves your praise.

GROUP DISCUSSION QUESTIONS

1. What is the difference between faith and belief?

2. What grade would you give your current level of faith? What grade would you give your current level of belief?

3. As you read this chapter, what is the Lord saying to you when it comes to building your belief?

4. How should you trust God for the outcomes of situations you are praying for in your life?

5. How do you have a *pro*active instead of a *re*active prayer life?

6. List the big prayers you are praying right now. Track when and how God answers these prayers.

SEVEN

Speak Life

Dead. Lifeless.

Not sleeping. Not resting.

Dead. Lifeless. *Hopeless.*

That is what Ezekiel saw. A dark valley filled with decrepit dead bones. God showed Ezekiel the gloomy scene and then asked, "Can these bones live?"

I have been in several hospital rooms staring at someone who was dead, lifeless and hopeless. Each time I felt that God was directing that same question at me: *Can these bones live?*

Perhaps right now you are looking at something that seems dead and, more than anything, you want it to live again.

Your marriage went from "romantic adventure" to "basically just roommates" to "life-support in the ICU" to "It's currently being rolled down to the morgue." You look at your marriage and wonder, *Can these bones live?*

You attend a church that you love, but fewer and fewer people are attending along with you. Members are moving away, and passing away, and not many new people are replacing them. You hate to admit it, but your church feels, well, dead. You wonder, *Can these bones live?*

You had a dream once, to start a business or to advance in your career or to go into ministry. Unfortunately, that dream has not taken a breath in years, and you wonder, *Can these bones live?*

My answer is *yes*. Dead bones *can* live again. I know it because I have seen it. But how does it happen?

God told Ezekiel,

> "Speak a prophetic message to these bones and say, 'Dry bones, listen to the word of the Lord! This is what the Sovereign Lord says: Look! I am going to put breath into you and make you live again! I will put flesh and muscles on you and cover you with skin. I will put breath into you, and you will come to life. Then you will know that I am the Lord.'"
>
> Ezekiel 37:4–6 NLT

Isn't that fascinating? God didn't ask Ezekiel to pray for the bones or to touch the bones. God told Ezekiel to *speak* to the bones. *Speak life to the bones, and they will live, and you will know that I am who I say I am and can do what I say I can do.*

That was more than 2,500 years ago. How does God resurrect dead things today? The same way He did back then—through words. We speak them to life.

Just Say the Word

In Luke 7 we read about a Roman centurion, a military officer, who sent people to Jesus asking if He would come and heal his valued servant. The men told Jesus that the situation was dire; the servant was near death. Jesus started walking toward the centurion's home but, just before they arrived at the house, the officer sent some friends to say, "Lord, don't trouble yourself by coming to my home, for I am not worthy of such an honor. I am not even worthy to come and meet you. Just say the word from where you are, and my servant will be healed. I know this because I am under the authority of my superior officers, and I have authority over my soldiers. I only need to say, 'Go,' and they go, or 'Come,' and they come. And if I say to my slaves, 'Do this,' they do it."

When Jesus heard this, he was amazed. Turning to the crowd that was following him, he said, "I tell you, I haven't seen faith like this in all Israel!" And when the officer's friends returned to his house, they found the slave completely healed.

Luke 7:6–10 NLT

This story absolutely amazes me because I didn't know Jesus could be amazed. But now that I know, I want to amaze Him!

What exactly amazed Jesus? The centurion's *faith*.

How did the centurion show his faith? How did Jesus become aware of his faith? Through *words*. The centurion sent a message of faith-filled words, and he asked Jesus to *just say the word*. This Roman official understood something I think a lot of Christians today don't. He knew Jesus did not have to come, did not have to see, did not have to touch; He just had to say the word. This centurion comprehended the power of words, telling Jesus, *I just say the word, and people obey me. If You just say the word, my servant will be healed.*

We need to understand the power of words.

Life and Death

God tells us, "The tongue has the power of life and death" (Proverbs 18:21), and "the words of the reckless pierce like swords, but the tongue of the wise brings healing" (Proverbs 12:18).

We speak, on average, about sixteen thousand words a day. I have no idea how many words we typically *hear* each day, but I think we can all attest to the power of words. Words can ruin marriages. Words can make a workplace toxic. Words can divide churches. As a pastor, I have counseled people who are still being controlled by words spoken to them by their parents decades ago.

Why is that?

God has hardwired the power of words into the universe.

In the first chapter of the Bible we see God speak the world into creation. How did God create? He used words.

In Genesis 3 we see Satan speak deception to Adam and Eve. It was words that caused the fall of man. The words were not true, but that did not take away their power.

In John 1 we are introduced to Jesus, and what is He called? "The Word." Then the unbelievable happens: The Son of God is conceived. Through the Holy Spirit, in the womb of Mary. And how is it described? "The Word became flesh and made his dwelling among us."

We learn quickly that Jesus came to bring heaven to the world, and the world to heaven, and His plan for doing that was . . . words: "Jesus [said], 'Let us go somewhere else—to the nearby villages—so I can preach there also. That is why I have come'" (Mark 1:38); "The Spirit of the Lord is on me, because he has anointed me to proclaim good news to the poor. He has sent me to proclaim freedom for the prisoners and recovery of sight for the blind, to set the oppressed free, to proclaim the year of the Lord's favor" (Luke 4:18–19).

We see Jesus use words to bring healing, stop a storm and raise the dead. *Peace, be still* or *Lazarus, come out*—that's all it took for Jesus to perform whatever miracle was needed in the moment.

More than 2,500 years ago God told Ezekiel to speak life to dead bones.

About 2,000 years ago Jesus spoke life to a centurion's dying servant.

Just a few years ago John Smith lay on a table in an emergency room, dead. The doctors had done everything they could do, but nothing was bringing this dead boy back. Then Joyce Smith walked in and spoke life. As God commanded Ezekiel, she spoke a prophetic message declaring that the Sovereign Lord was saying He would put breath into John and make him live again. And, to the astonishment of a room full of doctors, John came back to life.

As John stayed in the hospital for the next few weeks, Joyce and I enforced the decision that we, and anyone in John's presence, would speak *only* life. We were believing God for a miracle and were positioning ourselves for it by filling John's room with words of life and *not* allowing words of death.

Shouting Life

One time my wife and I went on vacation in Hawaii with two other couples. The three husbands had an early flight on our last day, leaving our wives, who were flying home that evening. They were spending their extra day exploring when my wife had to use the bathroom. (Paula *always* has to use the bathroom.)

They saw a Chevron station and stopped. The bathroom was across the parking lot from the convenience store, in its own little building. Paula ran up and tried the bathroom door, but it was locked. She figured she needed a key, so she ran over to the convenience store.

The attendant, a large Hawaiian woman, seemed confused. "It's still locked? That guy must have left it locked when he left." Apparently, it had been a long time since a young man had gone into the bathroom.

They walked across the parking lot together. The woman unlocked the door, recoiled in shock, and exclaimed, "Oh, dear Jesus—he's sleeping," and started to shut the door.

Paula realized something was wrong, grabbed the door and pulled it open.

She saw a man in his early twenties. (Paula and her friends refer to him as "Chevy.") (You know, because he was at a Chevron station.) Chevy was lying on the floor, head on the toilet, mouth wide open. His skin was gray and mottled. In his left hand was drug paraphernalia. Paula and her friends are not trained medical experts, but it seemed obvious to everyone that this guy was dead and had been dead for who knows how long.

Paula's two friends started praying, and Paula began speaking life. Actually, she began *shouting* life.

"You breathe now!" she shouted to the corpse. "Do you hear me? Breathe!"

The young man immediately took a long, shallow breath.

Paula yelled, "That's right! You breathe again!"

Chevy took another breath. For the next minute or so, Paula continued to speak life into him, commanding him with reliance on the authority and power of our God who, in the beginning, breathed life into Adam. Chevy continued taking breaths. His skin color started to transform from grayish purple to a healthy pink.

At that point Paula heard sirens. The convenience store worker had called 911, and the ambulance was getting close. Finally, it pulled up, and one of the paramedics jumped out and went to Chevy.

He put a hand on him, and Chevy looked up and said, "Hey! What are you doing?" Chevy was definitely alive and seemed to be doing well as they loaded him into the ambulance.

Why? I think it is because when Paula was confronted with a dead guy lying in a toilet, her automatic response was *not* to say, "Oh, no, he's dead," but to speak words of life.

Words That Flow

Now that you understand more about positioning yourself for a miracle, you're ready for two pivotal ideas that will equip you for a breakthrough.

Filling Your Heart

Here is a fact: When we encounter unforeseen circumstances or scary situations, words are going to flow—if not out of our mouths then through our thoughts. In a crisis (remember, every miracle starts with a crisis), these thoughts don't get cleaned up first; they reveal what we believe.

Jesus tells us why we can't run these words through filters: "What you say flows from what is in your heart" (Luke 6:45 NLT). When words come out, Jesus tells us they flow out directly from what is inside. The words that come pouring out of our mouths come from what is already stored away. When Paula saw Chevy, she didn't stop to think of appropriate words to fit that bizarre situation; the words of life just flowed.

So if we find ourselves saying, "She's going to die" or "I know my son will never come back to the Lord" or "I'm never going to be good enough" or "This isn't going to work" or "We'll never get out of debt," we are just revealing what we have already stored in our hearts.

Which leads to the first crucial point: *We need to fill our hearts with God's words.*

In Psalm 119:11 we read, "I have hidden your word in my heart that I might not sin against you." We need to have God's words in residence, so that, when crisis hits, His words flow out. See, what I am suggesting is not a prosperity, blab-it-and-grab-it gospel. We are not speaking what we want; we are speaking God's Word. God's Word is the "word of life" (Philippians 2:16). We

97

position ourselves for a miracle by holding firmly to the Word of life and proclaiming God's promises.

God is waiting for someone to take Him at His word. When we stand on the promises of God we can expect Him to fulfill them. Jeremiah tells us, "The LORD said to me, 'You have seen well, for I am watching over my word to perform it'" (Jeremiah 1:12 ESV). God is watching over His word of life and is ready to perform what He has promised.

That is why I would encourage you to memorize some key Bible verses. Write them down on 3x5 cards, put them in your pocket, and when you are standing in line or waiting at a red light, pull them out and read them. Read them until they are hidden in your heart.

The first pivotal point, then, is one of preparation—to fill our hearts with God's Word because we cannot choose what will come pouring out from our hearts in a crisis.

Guarding Your Heart

Putting yourself in position for a breakthrough to your miracle is not only about making sure the right things are in your heart; it's also about keeping the wrong things out. This will only happen because of a day-to-day decision.

In Proverbs 4 we are given this challenge: "Above all else, guard your heart, for everything you do flows from it" (Proverbs 4:23). In Hebrew culture, the heart was considered to be the core of a person. The Hebrew word for *heart* means literally "the kernel of the nut." The heart is the core of who we are.

The second crucial point, then, is this: *Above all else we need to guard our hearts*, because words flow from our hearts, and our words have the power of life and death.

What would it look like for you to guard your heart?

In that fourth chapter of Proverbs, and throughout the Bible, *priority is placed on what our ears hear*—on what and whom we are listening to. Why? Because our ears are a pathway to our hearts. What we hear flows into our hearts and will eventually flow out of our mouths in words of life or death. We are told to tune our ears to wise words and to "keep them within your heart; for they are life to those who find them and health to one's whole body" (Proverbs 4:21–22).

What are you listening to? Do you spend time with faith-filled friends who remind you of God's promises? Do you make it a priority to be at church and read your Bible so you are regularly hearing the Word of God? Do you listen to worship music, especially worship music that focuses not on your needs, but on the character of God?

Or do you spend time with negative friends who gossip and complain and barrage you with all that is wrong about your situation instead of what is right about God? Do you prioritize watching TV and reading romance novels? Do you listen to music that accentuates the temptation to be cynical or to seek life outside of God?

There are also cautions given in Proverbs 4 about *what our eyes see*: "Let your eyes look straight ahead; fix your gaze directly before you" (verse 25). I have heard that we remember about eleven percent of what we hear but about eighty percent of what we see. It is easy to think, *I can watch this show, I can look at this website because it's just looking, I haven't* done *anything*. No. What we see is also a gateway to our hearts, so we need to protect our eyes.

Don't allow yourself to listen to or look at anything that is counter to God's Word. Remember, words have the power of life and death.

Your marriage is struggling? Choose not to speak—not to give life to—the word *divorce*. In our house we don't even use the word. In faith, choose to speak only words of life: "I believe that God is going to heal our marriage and give us a better relationship than we've ever had."

A loved one is in a terrible accident? Choose not to speak the words *I think he's going to die*. In faith, speak only words of life. "We believe God is going to restore him to full health."

You are applying for a job or a promotion, but there are other qualified candidates? Choose not to speak words of defeat like *I know I won't get it*. In faith, choose to speak only words of life: "God is who He says He is and can do what He says He can do. I know He is for me, and I know He has good plans for me. He will give me this job if this job is His will for me."

If you find that negative words still rise to the surface in your mind, keep on soaking in God's Word and trusting His promises. Things will change. A good way to help this process along is to turn those negative words into thanksgiving and begin praising God for all that He has done in your life. You can't praise and entertain negative thoughts at the same time.

Psychologists talk about the law of exposure. It says that we will absorb, and our lives will reflect, whatever we are exposed to the most. Some of us are living lives God never meant for us to live, lives we don't want to live, because of what we have allowed into our hearts. We need to ask God to do some heart surgery.

Good news: He does that kind of thing! In fact, in the chapter before Ezekiel sees the valley of dead bones, God makes an offer to him and us: "I will give you a new heart and put a new spirit in you; I will remove from you your heart of stone and give you a heart of flesh. And I will put my Spirit in you and move you to follow my decrees" (Ezekiel 36:26–27).

You will discover that when you have God's Word in you, not only will it flow out of you when a crisis hits, but it will also help you see things more clearly. Typically, when circumstances turn us upside down, our responses are dictated by our feelings. Feelings are *not* a good barometer of reality. God's Word *is*. It is a true basis for an accurate assessment of the crisis.

Dead Bones Live

That is what Ezekiel discovered. God showed him the valley of dead bones and asked, "Can these bones live?"

Ezekiel assessed the situation then gave a feelings-based answer: "Sovereign Lord, you alone know."

God told Ezekiel to speak life over the dead bones so that "you will know that I am the Lord."

And next? Ezekiel tells us:

> So I prophesied as I was commanded. And as I was prophesying, there was a noise, a rattling sound, and the bones came together, bone to bone. I looked, and tendons and flesh appeared on them and skin covered them, but there was no breath in them.
>
> Then he said to me, "Prophesy to the breath; prophesy, son of man, and say to it, 'This is what the Sovereign Lord says: Come, breath, from the four winds and breathe into these slain, that they may live.'" So I prophesied as he commanded me, and breath entered them; they came to life and stood up on their feet—a vast army.
>
> Ezekiel 37:7–10

I don't know the situation you are facing, but I know I have stared at the dry bones of a dead boy, dead marriages, dead churches, people dead in their sins or addictions, and I have asked, *Can these bones live again?*, and the answer is always yes.

God calls me, and God calls you, with the authority of Jesus, to command: "Dry bones, listen to the word of the Lord! This is what the Sovereign Lord says." And then you speak life, and you keep speaking life, and you invite Jesus to "just say the word," and you watch as the Spirit breathes His fresh breath into your situation, and you see what was dead come back to life.

And when that happens? You will know that God is the Lord.

CONNECT WITH GOD

God, You created the world with words. You did miracles with words. You tell me that my words will flow out of what is in my heart, and will have the power of life and death. Please help me fill my heart with Your words, guard my heart and always speak words of life. I pray in the name of Jesus, whom You call "the Word," Amen.

POSITION YOURSELF

1. Start to pay attention to the words you hear. Are they positive or negative? Wise or unwise? Do they make you feel more alive or suck the life out of you? What needs to change about what you listen to?

2. Start to pay attention to the words you speak. You might begin your day by asking God to help you speak only words of life. Then monitor what comes out of your mouth. Ask God to give you discernment to know what it tells you about the condition of your heart.

3. Commit to memorizing some Bible verses; storing God's Word in your heart will help you be positioned for a miracle! Here are some suggestions:

"Purify yourselves, for tomorrow the LORD will do great wonders among you" (Joshua 3:5 NLT).

The words of the reckless pierce like swords, but the tongue of the wise brings healing (Proverbs 12:18).

"I tell you the truth, anyone who believes in me will do the same works I have done, and even greater works, because I am going to be with the Father" (John 14:12 NLT).

"If you remain in me and my words remain in you, ask whatever you wish, and it will be done for you. This is to my Father's glory, that you bear much fruit, showing yourselves to be my disciples" (John 15:7–8).

For if, while we were God's enemies, we were reconciled to him through the death of his Son, how much more, having been reconciled, shall we be saved through his life! (Romans 5:10).

Now to him who is able to do immeasurably more than all we ask or imagine, according to his power that is at work within us, to him be glory in the church and in Christ Jesus throughout all generations, for ever and ever! Amen (Ephesians 3:20–21).

And I am certain that God, who began the good work within you, will continue his work until it is finally finished on the day when Christ Jesus returns (Philippians 1:6 NLT).

God has not given us a spirit of fear and timidity, but of power, love, and self-discipline (2 Timothy 1:7 NLT).

GROUP DISCUSSION QUESTIONS

1. How did Jesus become aware of the centurion's bold faith?
2. What kind of power does your tongue have? Do you generally think about the power of your words in that way? Does it have any impact on the way you talk?

3. What do you think it means to "speak life"? Is this a new concept for you? What impact could it have on your life moving forward?

4. What amazed Jesus about the centurion's faith? How can we have that kind of faith today?

5. What kind of role does the heart play in what comes out of your mouth? If you look at what has been coming out of your mouth, does it line up with God's Word and His promises?

EIGHT

Surround Yourself

When you are in a crisis, it can be all consuming. John Smith was in the hospital, fighting for his life after an hour of death. We rarely left his side as we battled for him in prayer. For a while we had no idea of the crisis that was happening in the room next to John's.

Jackson, an adorable little three-year-old boy, was in that room. Jackson had come down with the flu. No big deal, right? Every kid gets the flu at some point. But a rare and mysterious side effect had paralyzed Jackson. He had been in the room next door for three weeks, and the doctors could not figure out the problem. In fact, Jackson's condition was growing worse. The paralysis had started in his feet, and was moving up his body, now finally affecting his neck and leaving him barely able to breathe. The doctors were in a race against time. Jackson was being prepped for emergency surgery that would hopefully keep his air passages open. Without help, he would die.

Jackson's parents, Chris and Leann Suhling, were believers, but they were a five-hour drive from home and their church family.

We were only a forty-minute drive from home, which meant we had a big crowd of friends filling the pediatric ICU waiting room with prayers and support. Chris and Leann had no one.

Let me ask you: What was the issue Chris and Leann were facing? You might say it was the flu. In a sense, sure, the flu was making their son sick. But I'm not so sure the flu was the real crisis. God can heal the flu easier than I can shoo a fly. Getting rid of Jackson's flu and its side effects would be easy for God.

The issue also was not faith. They were believers and believed God could heal their son.

The real issue was that they were all by themselves.

When we are in crisis, doubts can creep in, our hearts can wander. All by yourself is a dangerous place to be. To position ourselves for a miracle we need faith *and* friends. We need to surround ourselves with faith-filled friends.

Digging Through Rooftops

One of my favorite miracles that Jesus performed happened only because of some faith-filled friends. In Luke 5 we read about a man who was paralyzed. He had to live his life lying on a mat. Being paralyzed meant this man could do nothing for himself. He had to depend on someone else to feed him, clothe him, bathe him, carry him and take care of his . . . personal hygiene needs. This man was utterly incapable physically; he was completely dependent on others.

He was also hopeless, because at that time there was nothing that could be done for him—no surgeries or physical rehab. He would have to lie on his mat forever. That was his life.

As bad as it was for him physically, there were other devastating issues. In the ancient world people with physical defects were viewed as dispensable or worse. Historians believe the Greeks usually disposed of newborns if they had physical defects. In fact, the Greek philosopher Aristotle wrote: "Let there be a law that no deformed child shall be raised to adulthood." The Romans did just that. In the fifth century they had a statute that read: "Quickly kill a deformed child."

There were also spiritual issues for this man. In that day, people believed physical suffering was brought on by sin. Suffering was punishment from God.

So this man was thought of as different, less than, useless and supposedly cursed by God; yet somehow he was surrounded by an amazing group of friends. These friends wanted, more than anything, for their paralyzed buddy to be healed. They heard about Jesus and His power and realized the way to position their friend for a miracle was to get him close to Jesus. So they informed their friend that the next day they would come by to pick him up and take him to Jesus. (We don't know if he shared their faith in Jesus, but, either way, he had no choice but to go. Because when his friends picked him up, they *really* picked him up.)

The next day the man and his friends all arrived at the house where Jesus was, only to find it completely packed with people who also wanted to get close to Jesus. There was absolutely no way in. In fact, a crowd of people surrounded the house trying to catch a glimpse of Jesus or hear what He was saying. So not only could they not get in the house; they could not even get close.

No one would blame them if, at this point, they just gave up. The journey to get the man there was difficult enough. Now they couldn't even get to Jesus. They had good intentions, but things were not turning out the way they hoped. But, no, this group of friends was not about to give up. Their buddy needed a miracle, they believed Jesus could do it, and they were going to find a way.

I once heard pastor John Ortberg wonder in a sermon if maybe at this point they had a little brainstorming session, the natural leader of the group passionately getting everyone's attention. The friends did what guys do best: They got to work at solving the problem.

"Guys, we have to find a way. So let's brainstorm. And remember, when you brainstorm, there's no such thing as a bad idea."

Then they all probably just stared at each other for a long time.

Finally, someone spoke up. "Well, this is crazy, but . . . could we carry him up to the roof of the house? And could the four of us dig through the roof of the house? And could we somehow lower him down, through the roof, to Jesus?"

More blank stares.

Then the leader-type probably said, "Well, it turns out there *are* bad ideas in brainstorming, and that's one of them. We could drop him and kill him. Just getting him up to the roof would be a huge ordeal. Once we got up there, we could fall and kill ourselves. We could get arrested for destruction of property. Jesus might think we're idiots. What other ideas do we have?"

But there were none. So, they decided to go with the lower-him-through-the-roof strategy.

I wish I could have witnessed them getting their paralyzed friend to the roof. Imagine the new perspective this man would have had on life. Just think: More than likely he had never seen the world from this vantage point. It was a crazy thing to do. There was the risk of their friend falling, of them falling, but *faith* will do crazy things. Faith-filled *friends* will do crazy things.

I also would have loved to see them digging through the roof, hoping the owner of the house didn't have any major issues with vandalism.

Most of all, I would have loved to see the people *in* the house, as flakes from the ceiling started to descend, and they looked up and saw a crack, and, emerging through the crack, lots of fingers. As everyone stared, bewildered, the hole grew larger and finally four smiling faces appeared.

Two Kinds of Healing

Once the hole was big enough, they "lowered him on his mat through the tiles into the middle of the crowd, right in front of Jesus. When Jesus saw their faith, He said, 'Friend, your sins are forgiven'" (Luke 5:19–20).

I love it that they came hoping for a physical healing, but Jesus addressed the more important issue of the man's *spiritual* condition. Isn't it just like God to give us what we *need*, not just what we ask for? Jesus forgave the man's sins, which is the greatest need of *everyone*.

But Jesus wasn't done yet. A moment later, he said to the paralyzed man,

> "I tell you, get up, take your mat and go home." Immediately he stood up in front of them, took what he had been lying on and went home praising God. Everyone was amazed and gave praise to God. They were filled with awe and said, "We have seen remarkable things today."
>
> Luke 5:24–26

I wonder if it was a Tuesday, because they got the "Two for Tuesday" special: a spiritual *and* a physical healing. I love that!

I also love that it says, "When Jesus saw *their* faith." Whose faith did he see? Not *his* faith. *Their* faith. It was the faith of the friends that got the man to Jesus. It was the faith of the friends that positioned the man for the miracle he needed. If he had not surrounded himself with the right friends, he would never have gotten to Jesus, never have gotten healed physically, never have heard Jesus tell him his sins were forgiven. Without his friends, this miracle never would have happened.

Who's Carrying You to Jesus?

When I read this story, I think about my friends, and I wonder about *yours*. Have you surrounded yourself with faith-filled friends? Do you have friends who will make sure you get to Jesus? And are you a friend like that? Do you surround others with faith and carry them to Jesus?

We tend to war against this, because we live in a fiercely independent DIY (do it yourself) culture; but real friendship means allowing our friends to carry us, and it means carrying our friends.

When we need help, when we need to share our burdens, when we need people to pray, there is something inside of us that thinks, *But I don't like to ask . . . I don't want to impose . . . I don't want to inconvenience anyone.* I understand that. I sometimes feel like that, too. But real friends allow their friends to carry them and, if not, they are *not* real friends.

Think about the guy in this story. He must have felt bad about being totally dependent. He must have felt useless and vulnerable being carried everywhere every day. He must have been tempted to tell his friends, "No. I appreciate the offer, but I don't want you to carry me to Jesus." If he had given in to that temptation, no miracle.

So do you let your friends carry you? Do you ask? Do you show them your weaknesses and struggles? And are *you* the kind of friend who gives people the confidence that you will carry them? Do people ask you? Do they show you their weaknesses and struggles?

I hope you have friends like that. We all need to surround ourselves with faith-filled people. When the same bad physical condition has been plaguing you for too long, when the wine runs out at the party, when you are told you can stop asking Jesus now because your son is dead, doubts will creep in and seek to overtake your mind. You will be tempted to wonder if Jesus is asleep in the boat and if it is always going to be this way. You will find yourself praying the "If You can" and "Don't You care if I drown?" kinds of prayers. *That* is when your friends loan you their faith, speak life into your faith, and snap you back into a faith-centered perspective on your situation.

Do you have friends like that? You know you have the right friends by how you feel after you have been with them. Does spending time with your friends bring you down or make you feel uplifted?

You also know you have the right friends by what comes out of their mouths, especially when you are seeking a miracle. Do they share God's wisdom or their own opinions? Do they have a faith-fueled, God-centered positivity? Or do they speak negative thoughts that intensify your doubts?

My wife is one of my faith-filled friends who carry me to Jesus. Whenever I start feeling anxious, she snaps me out of it.

Some years ago, I was talking to our denomination's head-quarters about taking a position with them. When the pastor of the church where I was working found out, he told me, "You're done." He said I could have some time, but since I was looking elsewhere, my future was not with his church.

I put in my resignation the next day, giving thirty days' notice so there would be plenty of time for the church to fill my spot. We put our house on the market, and seven days later it sold. We put an offer on a house in the area where we would be moving, and it was accepted.

And *that* is when I was told that the job with the denomination might not be approved. I had a wife and four kids. In a few weeks we would have to move out of our house with nowhere to go. In a few months we would have to start making payments on the house we had just purchased, but it didn't look as though we would be moving there, so I would be paying for a house we might never live in.

I'm going to be honest with you: I freaked out. (Perhaps not what you want to hear from the guy writing the book on how to have faith that produces miracles, but it's true.) I was embarrassed but decided to be vulnerable and tell my wife how I was feeling. I felt paralyzed by fear, and I needed someone to carry me to Jesus. She did. Her faith and her words of life totally snapped me out of my fear.[1]

Do you have faith-filled friends like that? When you're stuck, lying on your mat, and you feel as if you can't move, do you have people who carry you to Jesus?

If you *don't* have anyone like that, you *need* someone like that. I'll say it again: All by yourself is a dangerous place to be. To position ourselves for a miracle we need faith *and* friends. We need to surround ourselves with faith-filled friends.

So what do you do if you don't have anyone like that? You pray for someone like that.

Singing from the Rooftops

Jackson was paralyzed, and his parents, Chris and Leann, were heartbroken. Jackson couldn't breathe. He was going in for emergency surgery, and his parents were all alone.

They were all alone *until* they met Joyce in the hallway. Joyce had left John's room for a moment, and she ran into Chris and Leann. She asked why they were in the PICU. They told her about Jackson, and about their faith, and about how far they were from their church family.

Joyce brought them to me and said, "Pastor, we need to pray with them!"

Suddenly, Chris and Leann *weren't* all alone. They were surrounded by faith-filled friends God brought them in their time of need. We went into Jackson's room together, and we held hands together, and we prayed together. Jesus tells us there is special power when two or more are gathered, praying in His name (see Matthew 18:20), and God's power showed up in a special way as we prayed.

I had to leave the hospital that afternoon for our Wednesday night service. As I was stepping onstage, Joyce sent me a video. The video was of Jackson . . . standing up in his bed, strumming his little toy Lightning McQueen guitar, and *singing*. Hours earlier he couldn't breathe, now he was singing!

Do you want to know what song he was singing?

"Rooftops" by Jesus Culture. He was belting out words about proclaiming Jesus' name from the rooftops!

I shared the video with our congregation, and they went nuts. (I still have it on my phone. Ask me and I'll show it to you when we meet!) I couldn't stop smiling. Not only because Jackson was healed, but because it made me think of those crazy, faith-filled friends. They were digging through a rooftop, praying for a miracle their friend was about to receive. Little Jackson? He was singing "Rooftops" celebrating the miracle he had just received.

CONNECT WITH GOD

God, we learn in the Bible that You have never been alone. You live in the community of Father, Jesus, Your Son, and Your Holy Spirit. We also learn, in the first pages of the Bible, that it is not good for man to be alone. God, I know I need You, and I need faith, but I also need friends. Would You please surround me with faith-filled friends who will give me Your strength when I am weak and who will carry me to Jesus? God, would You also help me to be that kind of friend to others? And thank You that Jesus calls me His friend. I pray in His name, Amen.

POSITION YOURSELF

1. If you were to grade yourself on a scale from 1 to 10 on how good a friend you are to others, what number would you give yourself? Consider: Do you share your faith with others? Do you speak life into your friends? Have you been carrying your friends to Jesus, especially when they are weak? What practical things can you do to improve your grade by a number or two?

2. If you were to grade yourself on a scale from 1 to 10 on how you are doing when it comes to surrounding yourself with faith-filled friends who bolster your faith and carry you to Jesus, what number would you give yourself? What practical things can you do to improve that grade by a number or two?

3. Commit to praying that you will be a better friend *and* surround yourself with better friends.

GROUP DISCUSSION QUESTIONS

1. Why is being all by yourself in a crisis dangerous?

2. What does it look like to walk beside a friend and help carry that one to Jesus?

3. We need to have the kind of tenacity to stand by our friends until they are healed. Sometimes that is hard. How can you develop that kind of tenacity?

4. Do you have friends in your life who are carrying you to Jesus?

5. If you don't have friends who will carry you to Jesus, what do you need to do?

6. Do you have friends who are pulling you away from Jesus? What do you need to do with those friendships? Will you?

NINE

Keep Your Eyes Open

Kim was in a desperate situation. For most of her life she had had Polycystic Kidney Disease (PKD). In PKD patients, hundreds of fluid-filled cysts develop within the kidneys. Over time they become larger and multiply, causing high blood pressure, chronic pain and eventual kidney failure. There are no treatments or medications offered for PKD patients. People with this disease have only two possible outcomes: a kidney transplant or death.

For 35 years Kim had regular appointments with her nephrologist to track and monitor this debilitating disease. After years of suffering she was running out of options and out of time. During an October visit with her doctor, he recommended that she start planning a visit to a hospital in St. Louis that specializes in transplants. The nephrologist did not recommend she begin dialysis while awaiting a possible transplant. It turned out to be a good thing that she never started dialysis, even though things became even more difficult without it.

Calls were made, and paperwork was filled out, seeking an immediate transplant. Kim then had to wait for several weeks finally to receive the word *Denied*. Mark was ready to give his kidney; he had planned from the moment Kim had been diagnosed that he would be donor. Kim was even denied for further evaluation. The doctors believed she was too high a risk and that her body would likely reject a new kidney.

This would have been a hope-killing setback for most, but not for Kim and Mark. They were not giving up that easily. They were disappointed, but still believed God had a miracle coming. With no hope for an organ transplant, Kim was given information on starting the dialysis process—but still she waited.

By late November Kim's doctors told her that her kidney function had dropped to fifteen percent. They told her that her kidneys weighed probably fifteen to twenty pounds each. They were so large they were filling her abdomen and squeezing her other organs. This was making it difficult for Kim to breathe, but she was grateful that she could still breathe at all.

Kim's skin was becoming jaundiced, and her hands and feet were constantly swollen. Her kidneys were filtering less and less, and her blood was getting more contaminated with higher levels of urine every day.

Kim's doctors sat her down and told her there was nothing else they could do. She had to have a kidney transplant to live, but because of risk and her certain incompatibility, she was not approved to have one. They were sorry, but they had no more answers for Kim. There was no hope.

Some People Brought a Blind Man

A certain man living in Bethsaida was in a desperate situation. We read in Mark 8 that some friends brought him to Jesus and begged Jesus to heal him. Again, we see the importance of surrounding yourself with faith-filled friends who get you to Jesus.

This guy was blind. We don't know if he was born blind or lost his sight later in life, but he could not see.

I wonder sometimes if we are blind. The Bible talks about people who can see, but are blind: "Like the blind we grope along the wall, feeling our way like men without eyes. At midday we stumble as if it were twilight; among the strong, we are like the dead" (Isaiah 59:10 NIV1984). The idea is we can struggle not only with physical but also with spiritual blindness.

For some, it's that they can't see their need for God. Their lives are working just fine without Him; they see no reason to seek Him or center their lives on Him.

For more of us, it's that we don't see how God is working. We are seeking a miracle, and God may already be answering our prayers, but we are blind to what He is doing. Sometimes our spiritual eyes are not open. Sometimes our spiritual enemy deceives us and keeps us from seeing God's work.

I think of when Elisha and his servant were surrounded by Aram's army. In 2 Kings 6:8–17 we read that the servant was afraid and cried out, "Oh no, my lord! What shall we do?"

Elisha had no fear. He said, with confidence, "Don't be afraid. Those who are with us are more than those who are with them." Then he prayed, "Open his eyes, LORD, so that he may see." Suddenly, the servant's eyes were opened, and he could see God's armies standing with them.

God was already providing a miracle; the servant was just blind to it. I wonder sometimes if we are blind to what God is doing.

Jesus Took the Blind Man by the Hand

Good news: We may be blind, but Jesus is really good at healing the blind. In the Bible, there are eight times when we see

Jesus heal the blind. Today, Craig Keener has traveled the world verifying reports of miracles and knows of 350 cases of people healed of blindness.[1]

The Bible says quite a bit about this. In Acts 26:18 Paul says his mission in life is to open people's eyes to spiritual truth. We are told in 2 Corinthians 3:16 that when we come to Christ, the veil is removed, and we see things we were not able to see before. We read in Ephesians 1:18 about God enlightening the eyes of our hearts.

That is good news because we can be spiritually blind and not see what God is doing. The blind guy just wanted to see again. His friends begged Jesus to heal him. I read that and, knowing how compassionate Jesus is, I cannot wait to read what happens next. I want to hear Jesus say, "Open your eyes and receive your sight." I want to see Jesus reach out and touch the man gently with His healing hands. But, no, the Bible says, "Then, spitting on the man's eyes . . ." (Mark 8:23 NLT). The guy has been struggling with blindness, he comes to Jesus, and Jesus spits on him! I don't know why, but it does show us that miracles are never "one size fits all." God is a creative Creator and is even an artist in how He does miracles. He healed another blind man with a word; here He used spit.

I wonder if maybe God takes different approaches so we will realize there isn't a blueprint He follows in doing miracles. God is sovereign, and we can't manipulate Him by trying to reproduce some formula we find in the Bible. There is no formula. If there were, we would probably end up trusting the formula instead of trusting God. There is no formula; there is a compassionate and powerful God who is unpredictable, but whom we are asked to trust.

The people in the Bible who experienced miracles didn't know exactly how God was going to do it, but they had faith that God could and would. They were not caught in the mechanics; they were caught up with a God who loved them and was coming through for them.

I think sometimes we miss what God is doing because He's not doing things the way we want Him to—so we think He's not doing anything at all. God *is* doing something; He is just not doing it the way we expect.

Healing in Stages?

Jesus spat on the man's eyes, touched him, then asked, "Can you see anything now?"

The man opened his eyes and said, "Yes. I see people, but I can't see them very clearly. They look like trees walking around."

Wait. Hold up. Did this miracle not quite work?

Look what happened next, "Then Jesus placed his hands on the man's eyes again, and his eyes were opened. His sight was completely restored, and he could see everything clearly" (verse 25 NLT).

This miracle happened in stages. It is the only time in the Bible we see this happen with Jesus healing someone.

We see it happening today. Candy Gunther Brown, who has an undergraduate degree, master's degree and doctorate from Harvard University, and is now a professor at Indiana University, studied the impact of intercessory prayer on healing. Taking an unbiased approach, she traveled the world doing clinical studies to determine if prayer really works.

Her conclusion? You guessed it: God is still in the miracle business.

Brown shares the story of Martine, an elderly blind and deaf woman in the Namuno village in Mozambique.[2] Before prayer, Martine had no response in either ear to sound measured at one hundred decibels. One hundred decibels is loud; that is the volume of a jackhammer. After prayer, she responded to

75 decibels in one ear and 40 in the other. After a second prayer, Martine's eyesight improved from 20/400 to 20/80. She had gone from being legally blind to seeing objects from twenty feet away as a person with normal vision would see them from eighty feet away. One prayer didn't do it. The miracle happened in stages.

I have been privileged to witness many miracles, and I have noticed that often God does His best work in stages. It's as though He puts together a bunch of little miracles to create the one big miracle for which the person is praying. I call it a tapestry of miracles. Sometimes to see the full healing we have to stand firm and fight for it. We have to stand on God's promises until we see it completed.

Consider this: John Smith and his two friends fell through the ice and . . .

A man nearby just "happened" to look out, see it happen and call 911.

The firefighters just "happened" to have had ice rescue training the previous week.

A first responder who was in the water trying to find John's body just "happened" to sense a nudge to look in the opposite direction.

That morning Joyce just "happened" to be reading the *Believing God* Bible study.

Joyce walked into the emergency room believing God, prayed and John's heart just "happened" to start beating again at that exact moment.

A drowning and hypothermia expert just "happened" to be John's doctor at the hospital where John was taken for critical care.

John swallowed tons of gross lake water that filled his lungs, but the tests revealed that his lungs just "happened" to be completely free from harmful bacteria.

And on and on. Everyone was praying that John would come back to life, stand up and walk out of the hospital in full health. That *is* what happened, but it happened piece by piece over the course of sixteen days. Because the big miracle we were seeking didn't happen immediately, some people doubted and thought God was not answering our prayers. He was. He just wasn't doing it the way they thought He should. He was doing it in stages. There were threads of miracles being woven together, one at a time, to form the full tapestry miracle we were seeking.

People ask me why God often does it like that. I don't know for sure, but I wonder if maybe God wants to grow our faith along the way. God always wants to take us to the next level. Perhaps we don't quite believe enough at the start, but as we see God doing His work, little by little, thread by thread, our belief in what God can and will do grows.

We need to keep our eyes open and not be blind to the little things. I encourage people to keep a journal, especially when they are praying for a miracle. I tell them to write down everything they are asking for, and everything they see God doing. As you witness God's activity, record it—all of it. You will find your belief growing.

Mike and RaeAnn

One morning as he began his workday, Mike fell over as he was about to get into his truck. His work partner discovered him and called 911. He then called Mike's wife, RaeAnn. RaeAnn called me.

I got to the hospital shortly after the family and learned that Mike had an extreme and deep brain bleed that had caused a stroke. This happened at the same time—the second week—that John Smith was in the hospital.

The doctors told RaeAnn they could not help Mike. In fact, the brain bleed was so severe, they had no hope he would survive. What made it worse was that Mike's father had died of exactly the same thing.

I sat down together with RaeAnn, their kids (all grown adults) and their extended family. I could see in everyone's eyes how scared they were, but I told them, "No. We won't give in to fear. We have faith. We are going to hold the line."

I was so proud of them because they did exactly that. Paula was there as well, and we all prayed together that God would astound the doctors by supernaturally healing Mike's brain. We prayed that Mike would walk out of the hospital with no adverse effects.

That's not what happened that day.

But two days after the stroke, Mike was out of the woods. Not dead as the doctors had predicted. He was alive and recovering.

The doctors called it a miracle, but they warned RaeAnn that Mike would never be the same and would never walk again. We prayed that Mike would spring out of bed and show them what God can do.

That's not what happened that day.

But eventually he could stand, with a cane. Then he could walk, with a cane. Then he could walk, without a cane.

Today, Mike is almost fully back to himself. Actually, he is better. God used what happened in a powerful way in Mike's life, and he is a changed man.

What I love is that RaeAnn and the kids and the entire family kept their eyes open. They saw what God was doing and celebrated it, every step of the way.

Mike's work partner found him collapsed on the road. Thank You, Jesus!

Mike is going to live! God did it!

Mike can stand with a cane! Yay, God!

Mike can walk with a cane! God is so good!

Mike can walk without a cane! Jesus healed him!

Instead of questioning why God was not doing what they wanted the way they wanted when they wanted, RaeAnn and the kids trusted and took note of everything God was doing along the way. Their belief grew as they kept their eyes open and saw God answering their prayers, even if it was not what they expected or when they expected it.

That is the way it tends to work.

Sometimes God even starts doing the miracle long before we know we need it. That brings us back to Kim.

Kim's Kidneys

The doctors told Kim there was no hope. The only thing that could save her was a kidney transplant, but she was too sick to receive one.

The doctors knew Kim's condition, but they didn't know Kim.

Kim is a woman of faith who was trusting God for a healing. She and Mark attended our church, and every Sunday and Wednesday she was the first one at the altar—praying and speaking words of life over her ailing kidneys.

"God is so faithful!" she would say. "I know He's going to heal me. I know He has this in His hands. God is with me right now. He is walking with me." Never, no matter how dire the reports from the doctors, did Kim speak a negative word. She spoke life, believing her "dead" kidneys would "live again."

One day Mark, feeling a leading from God, got in contact with the Mayo Clinic in Rochester, Minnesota, and made an appointment to see a specialist. He wanted another opinion. They drove 450 miles so Kim could have more tests and evaluations.

That was one of the tapestry threads. They learned that no one gets an appointment at Mayo without a referral. When the specialists realized Mark and Kim had secured an appointment on their own with no referral, they were shocked.

The specialists at Mayo confirmed Kim's need for a transplant. Her kidneys were now functioning less than ten percent. An immediate transplant was the only chance she had to live, and, at best, she would be placed at the bottom of a long list. Then Mark's own offer of a kidney was denied because they discovered that he had only one kidney that functioned normally. This was a blow to Mark because now he couldn't help his wife. At that moment things looked very bleak.

When I heard that her only chance was an immediate transplant, which seemed out of the question, I felt as if someone had punched me in the stomach. When I heard that Mark couldn't be the donor, that was another hit. Our church had been praying, and I had been expecting good news.

But Kim continued to hold on to her hope in Jesus.

One day as Kim's time was running dangerously close to the end, Chad, Kim's 34-year-old son, said he wanted to be tested as a possible donor. Because PKD is hereditary, he had never been considered. Chad had not shown any symptoms of PKD, and he felt certain God was telling them that he would be the donor.

Kim was deeply moved by this. She admitted that she feared what a test might reveal about his own health. And she was uncertain he would even be a match; the odds were not in their favor. And if he was a match, how would the loss of a kidney affect him? But she still trusted God, and Chad went up to Mayo.

The news came back immediately: Chad was a perfect match and had no trace of PKD. A miracle.

When Kim arrived for surgery, her pre-testing revealed her kidney function was now at less than one percent. The surgery, which was supposed to take twelve hours, went so smoothly it lasted only eight. When the doctors took Kim's kidneys out of her body, they were the size of footballs and indeed weighed twenty fluid-filled pounds each.

Today, three years later, Kim is completely healed and feels better than she ever has. Chad rebounded immediately and ran a full marathon within a year of his life-saving gift.

The other concern facing Kim and Mark was how they would pay for the surgery and all the medical attention. Imagine how she felt when the Mayo Clinic told her she has a rare benefit in her health insurance that covers one hundred percent of organ transplant surgery, including all lodging and travel and follow-up appointments. Another miracle!

Many people were astounded by it all, but not Kim. She had trusted God and spoken life. God proved trustworthy and gave her life.

Want to hear the *first* miracle in this process? Thirty-four years earlier, Kim had a last-minute emergency C-section at Chad's birth. That is what led to the discovery of Kim's kidney issue. The doctors told her that if they had known about her PKD they would have cautioned her against continuing the pregnancy. She should not even have been able to conceive a child with her condition, and her pregnancy probably should have killed her. But that child to whom she gave life was the very one God used to give her a second chance at life.

God saved Kim's life in stages, and the first stage happened decades before she even knew she needed a miracle.

CONNECT WITH GOD

Father, You have healing power in Your hands and, I learn today, even in Your spit! Miracles are not hard for You. Grow my belief in Your ability to do the impossible in my life.

God, sometimes maybe I have expectations of how You should do things and when You should do things. But You are sovereign, and You are creative. I need to trust what You are doing, however and whenever You choose to do it.

Please open my eyes and help me to see and be grateful for Your work in my life. Help me to notice everything You are doing. Thank You! I pray in Jesus' name, Amen.

POSITION YOURSELF

1. Read Mark 8:22–26. What do you note about this miracle? What surprises you? Why do you think Jesus did all the things He did? How does it apply to your life?

2. Think about difficult situations you have gone through in the past. How did God work in those situations? Is it possible God did some things for you that you might have missed because they were not the things you were asking for or expecting?

3. Start a prayer/miracle journal. Commit to writing down what you are asking God for and every way God answers. Record when God answers your requests in the way and timing you are seeking, but also write down everything else you see God doing, even if it is not what you expected or is "smaller" than the miracle you are asking for.

GROUP DISCUSSION QUESTIONS

1. Why is it important to remember that God's timing might be different from your timing?

2. How might a "veil" be covering your eyes? How can you lift it?

3. When you look back over your life, what are some of the miracles you have seen and experienced?

4. Jesus healed the blind man in stages. How can you keep your eyes open so you see what God is doing?

5. What is the most important thing you can do while you are waiting for a miracle?

TEN

Do Battle

Did you see the movie *Edge of Tomorrow*?

Tom Cruise plays Major William Cage, who looks like a hero, but isn't. Technically, he is a soldier, but he is one who sits behind a desk. He hasn't seen battle a day of his life.

We learn quickly that earth is at war against invaders from another planet. These aliens are attacking and seem impossible to defeat.

Cage is asked to take a camera crew to the battlefront. He refuses. He doesn't go to battlefronts. He doesn't fight.

Cage is arrested for disobeying orders and threatening his supervising officer. As punishment, he is sent to the frontlines to do battle with a unit stationed at Heathrow Airport in London. He is strapped into an exoskeleton weapon that he has not been trained to use. He is sent into battle but has no idea how to do battle. Within five minutes he is killed by an alien.

Just before he dies, he accidently releases the safety on his gun and shoots one of the aliens. Blood spills out of the alien and directly into Cage's open mouth.

Cage is dead.

Then he wakes up. He is alive again and it is the same day again. Somehow, he has gone back in time and is reliving the day when he was first put into the unit at Heathrow. Everything is exactly the same.

The only difference is Cage now possesses the knowledge he gained the day before.

He, again, goes into battle but this time knows how to switch off the safety on his gun. That helps but within about six minutes he is killed by an alien.

Cage is dead, again.

Then he wakes up, again. It the same day all over again, again. Everything is exactly the same, except Cage now possesses two days of knowledge about how to do battle.

He enters into the war against the aliens again, but this time he is better prepared because he has already practiced this day twice.

This happens over and over and over. Ten times, a hundred times. Each day a new day, but the same day, with Cage going into the same battle.

Each time he has more knowledge, more experience, and he knows better what to expect. Each day he is better equipped, because he has done battle for another day, so each day he experiences more success.

Legion

Major Cage looks stunned when he has to confront a crazy looking, terrifying alien. In the Bible, we see a time Jesus' disciples are stunned when they have to confront a crazy looking, naked, bloody, terrifying dude in a graveyard.

In Mark 5 and Luke 8, we read that Jesus and the disciples cross the Sea of Galilee. A horrible storm comes up. The storm is so bad the disciples are certain they are going to die. They wake up Jesus, who calms the storm. The disciples must be wondering: *What's so important that we need to cross the lake in this storm?* They are about to find out.

Jesus and His disciples get out of the boat, and this crazy guy comes running at them. He lives in the graveyard, where people try to bind him with chains. He is so strong he tears the chains apart. He never wears clothing. He cuts himself with stones and cries out all night and day.

Are you getting the picture? He is naked. He is bloody. He is strong and mean and horrifying, and he comes running at Jesus and the disciples. I wonder if they start thinking, *We didn't sign up for this!* They probably yell, "Let's get away from this monster!"

But Jesus might have calmly answered, "He's no monster. He is a man in misery. He's the reason we came. Today we're going to set him free."

The wild man falls at Jesus' feet and demands, "What do You want with me?"

Jesus asks his name, and he replies, "My name is Legion, for we are many."

Then Jesus does a miracle, casting the many demons out of him and into a herd of pigs.

The man is healed. He is finally free.

The pigs go charging down a hill and into a lake, where they drown. The townspeople show up, and they see this man who has been possessed by a legion of demons, now sitting, dressed and in his right mind. Instead of rejoicing, they are afraid. Sometimes change, even positive change, frightens people.

The townspeople also seem to be upset about the financial loss represented by the two thousand pigs floating in the lake.

They ask Jesus to leave their town.

Wow!

The guy who has been living in torment, and who had been tormenting the townspeople, must be totally confused. Why aren't they happy for him? Why aren't they happy for themselves and their now calmer, safer town?

As requested, Jesus gets into the boat to leave, and the healed man runs to Him and asks if he can come. It's a great request! So often Jesus asked people to follow Him; here was someone asking Jesus if he could follow. But Jesus says no.

He says to the man, "Stay, and tell everyone what I have done for you."

Right about now you might be wondering what a Tom Cruise movie and a story about a demon-possessed man have to do with you. The answer, of course, is *everything*.

When you start praying for a miracle, you are entering dangerous territory. Two thousand years ago, twelve guys said yes to following Jesus. What they signed up for was a spiritual battle so scary it made them want to run. I believe that's why the storm they encountered on the Sea of Galilee came up in the first place. The enemy knew why they were coming: to set a tormented man free. Once that tormented man was free his testimony would lead many to Jesus. The enemy was not concerned about the man's past; he was threatened by his future. The enemy would do anything to keep Jesus and the disciples away—including causing a storm. When we decide to follow Jesus today, we are agreeing to go to the battlefront and face an invading army.

This is so important, I want to walk you through it and make sure you clearly understand.

A Spiritual Battle, Fought in an Unseen World

There is a physical world that we are well aware of, but there is also an unseen world that we may be ignoring: "For we are not fighting against flesh-and-blood enemies, but against evil rulers and authorities of the unseen world, against mighty powers in this dark world, and against evil spirits in the heavenly places" (Ephesians 6:12 NLT).

The battle we are engaged in is spiritual, and it is being waged in the unseen world. There are examples of this in the Bible.

We see Daniel pray but receive no answer. Finally, an angel arrives with the answer and an explanation. The reason for the delay was a spiritual battle raging in the heavens: the angel was blocked from reaching Daniel.

Have you ever considered that your prayers are being influenced by spiritual forces warring against each other?

Remember Elisha and his servant as they face Aram's army? The servant is afraid. Elisha prays that his eyes be opened, and he is finally able to see that they are surrounded and supported by a great spiritual army.

Do you realize that you are not fighting alone?

This is not just in the Bible. Two times I have become aware of angels while praying for a miracle. Some people are surprised by that, but if the Bible is true we should expect it.

We see our issues as physical issues, and we treat the battle as a physical battle, but our problems are not really physical in nature. We are involved in a spiritual battle being waged in an unseen world.

And in this unseen world, you have an unseen enemy.

You have an enemy, and it's not a person. We are not fighting against flesh-and-blood enemies. Your enemy is not your mean boss or your ex-spouse or the parent who keeps nagging you or the guy who cut you off in traffic or the negative doctor or overbearing nurse.

Your enemy is Satan. Satan hates God and everything God loves. God loves you, so Satan hates you. He wants to prevent anything good from happening in your life, and he wants to take you out. Paul tells us to be aware of his schemes. What are they?

Satan will seek to blind you, keeping you from seeing, accepting or remembering God's truth.

He will seek to steal from you. His purpose is to steal, kill and destroy (see John 10:10).

He will seek to stop you. Paul wrote, "We wanted very much to come to you . . . but Satan prevented us" (1 Thessalonians 2:18 NLT).

He will seek to destroy you. "Your enemy the devil prowls around like a roaring lion looking for someone to devour" (1 Peter 5:8). He wants to destroy friendships, marriages, kids, health, finances and, most of all, our relationship with God.

How We Do Battle

It is only through our connection with God that we can do battle with the forces of darkness: "For though we live in the world, we do not wage war as the world does. The weapons we fight with are not the weapons of the world. On the contrary, they have divine power to demolish strongholds" (2 Corinthians 10:3–4).

We cannot fight this battle in our own power; we need God's power. The Bible encourages us to "be strong in the Lord and in his mighty power" (Ephesians 6:10).

God will give us the power to fight, and He loves us so much He has equipped us with spiritual armor for the battle. We are told, "Put on the full armor of God, so that you can take your stand against the devil's schemes" (Ephesians 6:11). Your spiritual enemy is scheming against you. He has a strategy he uses against you every day to keep you from God and the abundant life God has for you. To stand against this enemy, you need to put on your spiritual armor. What is your armor?

"Stand firm then, with the belt of truth buckled around your waist" (Ephesians 6:14).

You have the belt of truth. The way Satan attacks you is with deception, so you need to know God's truth. The enemy will lie and tell you that there is no hope, that it will never change, that what you are praying for is never going to happen. You need to know God's truth to overcome those lies.

"*. . . with the breastplate of righteousness in place*" (Ephesians 6:14).

Righteousness means you are right with God. If you have put your faith in Jesus and what He did on the cross for you, you are right with God.

The Bible says that the heart is deceitful above all things and will lie to you. This means that you might sometimes feel that you are not right with God—as though He is not with you. Your enemy loves to make you feel that way. That is why you *cannot* live by what you feel. You have to live by what you know.

You guard yourself with the breastplate of righteousness. If you have put your faith in Jesus, then you can be sure that God is for you, is listening to your prayers and will act on your behalf.

"*. . . and with your feet fitted with the readiness that comes from the gospel of peace*" (Ephesians 6:15).

You are unmovable because your feet are planted in the peace of God. This is not saying that life will always be peaceful; it is saying that you are resting in the peace that God is always in control. So, if you get a call from the hospital or the police, if the doctor gives you bad news, if the principal of your kid's school calls you in, you find you have peace that make no sense to you. It's because that peace comes from God. In the Roman world a soldier's shoes had spikes attached to the bottom to help hold the soldier in place. The shoes of peace will make us unmovable.

"In addition to all this, take up the shield of faith, with which you can extinguish all the flaming arrows of the evil one" (Ephesians 6:16).

Your enemy attacks you with flaming arrows. I find it interesting that back in Bible times, armies would march into battle in a preplanned, practiced alignment, almost like a marching band at halftime of a football game. The soldiers would typically wear armor made of leather. The enemy would shoot flaming arrows at the soldiers. Those arrows were not designed to kill; the intention was to set a soldier's leather armor on fire so that he would panic and break from formation. If he did, it could send the whole formation into chaos.

Your enemy is shooting flaming arrows at you. They might not kill you, but if he can make you panic, your fear could throw you into chaos.

That is why we have the shield of faith. The enemy fires his flaming arrows: "Your prayers won't work," "Your marriage will always be bad," "He won't get better," "You'll always be broke," "You'll always be sick," "God's not listening and won't come through for you."

Because of your faith, you know those are lies. You hold up the shield of faith and quench those flaming arrows by saying, "I do not believe what the enemy says; I believe what God says. God says He has plans to bless me and prosper me and to give me a hope and a future, and He is working in all things to bring about good for me, because I love Him and have been called according to His purpose."

"Take the helmet of salvation" (Ephesians 6:17).

Salvation means "to be saved." Knowing we are saved, that we have refuge in God and a future in heaven, should protect us from ever losing hope. Our minds need to be protected from the lies that the enemy is constantly throwing our way.

". . . and the sword of the Spirit, which is the word of God" (Ephesians 6:17).

Our offensive weapon is the sword of the Spirit, which is the Word of God, the Bible. If you don't know God's Word, at best you will struggle to fight back.

There is a scene in the Bible where we see Jesus being tempted by Satan: Guess how Jesus fought back? He responded to every temptation by quoting a verse from the Bible.

We need to be able to do the same. We need to know God's Word. To internalize God's Word. We fight just as Jesus did.

"And pray in the Spirit on all occasions with all kinds of prayers and requests. With this in mind, be alert and always keep on praying for all the Lord's people" (Ephesians 6:18).

Pray! That is how you engage in the battle; you pray. You pray because that is how you access God's divine power. You pray because that is how you put on the armor of God. You pray in the Spirit because when you do you are inviting God to break through and do a miracle.

There is a dark, unseen spiritual world where the battle is being waged. You have a spiritual enemy who is seeking to destroy you, to keep you from God and the life He has for you, to keep you from believing that God can work in your situation.

You have to do battle in the spiritual realm, with the power of God, protected by the armor God has given you.

If this is new to you, it might sound overwhelming. Even if this is not new to you, it probably should sound overwhelming. But there is good news. Two pieces of good news.

First, you have an enemy, and, yes, he is scary, but God is in you and is more powerful. Check out 1 John 4:4: "You belong to God, my dear children. You have already won a victory . . . because the Spirit who lives in you is greater than the spirit who lives in the world."

If you have invited God into your life, His Spirit is in you. And He is powerful. He is more powerful than your enemy. He is greater. And so, you can defeat your enemy. You can defeat your enemy as you keep your faith in and stay connected to God.

Second, if you are new to this, sure, it seems intimidating, and you are worried that you don't really know what you are doing in this battle. You might feel like Major William Cage in *Edge of Tomorrow*, who had no idea what to do when he went into battle in his new armor for the first time. But, remember, as he entered the battle again and again, each day becoming more familiar with his armor and better able to use it, he became increasingly more comfortable and successful.

The same is true for you. As you enter the battle you will go from feeling out of place and not knowing what to do, to feeling competent and knowing exactly what to do.

Just like Shara.

Shara

It was December 21, 2017. Shara was back at the hair school she owned in Port Angeles, Washington. Remember Shara? She is the one who called me when her husband, Dave, collapsed in their kitchen after inhaling insecticide—and was healed miraculously.

Shara had yelled into the phone, "We need you here! I don't know what to do!"

That was a couple of years earlier. On this cold winter morning Shara left home very early and headed for the hair school, taking special care on the icy roads. She arrived at 4:20 a.m., to be exact. She needed to do a few repairs at the school while no students were around.

Just about that time, a dad named Darrel was driving back home. He and his two kids had gone to see his mother, who was in a hospital in another city. Suddenly, not far from the hair school, he lost control of his minivan on the ice and crashed into an electrical pole.

A moment later Darrel sat dazed. The van was destroyed, twisted around the pole. Hearing no sounds from either of his boys, he thought they were dead. He looked around wildly and saw Shara's hair school. He knew her because she cut his sons' hair.

Darrel managed to dial her number and, when she answered, screamed, "I killed my boys!"

After a minute of confusion, Shara understood Darrel was outside, so she ran out and saw his van wrapped around the pole just down the road. She started running, falling several times on the icy street. One of the doors had been ripped off and she saw Andrew, Darrel's four-year-old son, in his car seat, which was hanging outside the van.

She finally reached Darrel, and he screamed, "I killed my boys!"

At that moment, Shara entered the battlefront. She put her hand over his mouth. "Darrel, stop! Don't you dare speak one more word like that. We're only going to speak life. Start praying *now*!"

Shara looked at the scene before her. The pole had fallen on the van and landed on Darrel's other son, fourteen-year-old

Ethan. The pole had broken every bone in Ethan's face. It had also crushed his clavicle, punctured his lungs, broken three of his ribs, shattered his pelvis, ruptured his femur and ripped open his aortic valve.

Shara immediately started praying for Ethan.

She managed to get Andrew out of his car seat. He had cuts across his body. She handed him to Darrel, saying, "Pray over him."

Shara went back to praying for Ethan. An ambulance showed up. An emergency medical technician (EMT) told Shara that Ethan was dead, and asked her to move away from the van.

Shara stood firm. "No!"

The EMTs were calling the time of death.

Shara insisted, "No!"

A guy came out of the nearby gym. He ran up and asked, "What can I do?"

Shara told him, "Get this pole off Ethan's head."

He managed somehow to reposition it, as Shara continued to pray. She prayed the prayers she had heard me pray back when Dave was about to die. She prayed the prayers that Joyce Smith and I had prayed when John was barely hanging on to life in the hospital.

"Give me this boy back, God. Holy Spirit, put Your breath in Ethan's lungs. I know You're going to do this, Father. I trust You!"

She prayed for ten minutes. The EMTs kept asking her to move aside so they could take care of Ethan's dead body.

Shara would yell at them, "No. I'm not doing it!" She continued to pray. She says it was the longest ten minutes of her life.

Suddenly, Ethan started spitting up blood.

"He's breathing!" she shouted to the EMTs.

They hurried over, saw it was true and jumped into action. They put a silver blanket over Ethan to help retain his body heat and set up the Jaws of Life, a hydraulic apparatus that could pry apart the metal around him so they could remove him from the van.

Shara continued to pray loudly as they worked, holding high the shield of faith. "We're gonna be all right, Ethan. God's got you. You're going to live. You're going to be all right."

The EMTs finally got Ethan out of the van, and put him and Andrew into an ambulance and rushed them to the hospital. Shara and Darrel arrived at the hospital just after them.

They were told the boys were about to be airlifted to Seattle, and that Darrel needed an MRI.

Shara went with Ethan and Andrew to the helicopter. Little Andrew was afraid.

He kept saying, "Don't leave me, Bubbles." (He could never remember Shara's name, so always called this lady who cut his hair "Bubbles.")

Nurses came to make the trip in the helicopter with Ethan and Andrew.

Shara said, "Are you my angels? Are you gonna take care of these boys? I need you praying the whole way." The helicopter took off.

Shara found Darrel, who was being released, and said, "Let's go to Seattle."

Before they left they were told, "Ethan's not going to make it."

Shara said no, she refused to believe that. God was going to heal Ethan.

When they arrived at the hospital in Seattle, Ethan was already in surgery and Andrew was being prepped and about to go in.

Shara learned that the doctor who was operating on Ethan was a nationally recognized, incredibly skillful surgeon. After the surgery, he explained to Darrel and Shara that there was no way Ethan should have survived, but somehow the open artery had scabbed up and closed. It wasn't possible, but it happened.

The pressure from the helicopter ride should have opened the artery back up, but that had not occurred.

Shara had learned from her husband's frightening experience to use everything the doctor told her to inform her prayer requests. Whatever the doctors said was wrong with Ethan and Andrew would be her guidance for prayer.

Shara started putting specific prayer requests on Facebook, and calling people, asking them to share what was happening on their own Facebook pages. Soon, people all over the world were praying for Andrew and Ethan, who was in a coma and on life support.

Shara and Darrel did not leave the hospital. Darrel was with his sons day after day, praying and trusting God, and Shara was there to back him up and be the friend who carried this family to Jesus in their time of greatest need. Christmas came and went, and Shara never left the boys. She stayed. She believed God for a miracle, speaking words of life, surrounding herself with faithful people, and praying specifically for each thing that was wrong with the children.

Little Andrew was progressing well, and dates began to be discussed regarding his discharge from the hospital. Ethan, however, appeared to be nonresponsive. At one point, at Ethan's bedside, a doctor told Darrel and Shara that the time had come to take Ethan off life support; it was time to say goodbye.

Shara told him he could not say that in front of Ethan.

The doctor assured her, "He's in a coma. He can't hear us."

Shara wasn't having it. "I don't care. You're not saying that in front of Ethan. We're only speaking words of life."

They all left the room together. The doctor said he was sorry, but they were going to pull the oxygen tube, and Ethan would not be able to breathe on his own.

Shara asked for five minutes alone in the room before they pulled the tube. She prayed, "Ethan, honey, when they pull the tube, you need to breathe like a lion. You're going to live, honey. God, You're the Master Creator. Put him back together. You can do this. I know You're going to do this."

The doctors came in and removed the life-support system.

Ethan breathed on his own.

The doctors said it wouldn't last.

Shara said, "Keep praying, Ethan. You breathe like a lion. God, put his bones back together. Put his muscles back together."

Ethan kept breathing.

Shara smiled and thanked God.

When medical personnel had first tried to insert the breathing tube, the bones around Ethan's sinus cavities were so broken up the tube could not be inserted normally. Shara prayed for Ethan's sinuses. When they took the tube out, the bones had somehow come back together.

Shara smiled and thanked God.

X rays at both hospitals showed that Ethan had a shattered pelvis. Shara repeatedly prayed that God would heal Ethan's pelvis. On the day that surgery was scheduled to repair it, Shara was in the cafeteria and saw a doctor she didn't recognize.

She asked, "Any chance you're the surgeon for Ethan today?"

He said, "Yes, I am."

She inquired, "What do you do for a shattered pelvis?"

The doctor looked confused. He explained that recent X rays showed only three small cracks in the pelvic area.

He assured her, "I'm doing a non-invasive surgery. We're just putting in a pin. It's no big deal."

She smiled and thanked God.

Ethan's shoulder and ribs were broken in the accident. Shara prayed God would heal them. The doctors later discovered that Ethan's shoulder and ribs had come back together.

Shara smiled and thanked God.

At this writing, not even a year after the accident, Ethan is walking and is about to start school. Little Andrew, after being sent home from the hospital, continued to recover well.

What I love about that story is that a couple of years earlier Shara had called me about Dave's desperate condition in an absolute panic. She had shouted, "I don't know what to do!" She had no idea how to do spiritual battle.

But when she rushed over to the accident scene and Darrel was screaming, "I killed my boys!" she knew exactly what to do.

In fact, when she was back home, Shara told me, "Now people call me!"

She had learned how to do battle.

You can, too.

One more thing: Remember how Jesus told the man who experienced the miracle in the graveyard to go and tell everyone what God had done for him? One of my other favorite things about Shara is that she is one of the most evangelistic people I know. She is constantly telling people about Jesus and inviting them to meet Him and put their faith in Him.

Shara understands, and the graveyard guy was about to experience, one of the highest purposes of miracles.

We are going to learn about it in the next chapter.

CONNECT WITH GOD

Lord, I see the physical world, and it's easy for me to focus on it. People cause me problems, and it's easy for me to think they are my enemies. But God, I know the truth. There is an unseen world, and that is where the battle is. Help me always to remember that. I have an unseen enemy. God, I reject Satan. Help me to know the truth so I can always overcome his lies. God, I need to be wearing my spiritual armor. Thank You for providing it. Please don't let me go a day without being in my armor, ready to defend myself against the devil's schemes. And help me to know and remember Your Word so I'm ready to use the sword of the Spirit. God, no matter what I face, lead me to be alert and to pray in the Spirit. In Jesus' name, Amen.

POSITION YOURSELF

1. Think about your struggles. Do you tend to view them as physical or spiritual? Do you see your enemy as a flesh-and-blood person or Satan? When you encounter difficulties, do you consider the possibility that they are part of Satan's strategy to steal from, kill and destroy you?

2. Do you intentionally put on the armor of God every day? How could you make, through prayer, putting on each piece of armor in Ephesians 6, a part of your regular morning ritual? What difference do you think that would make?

3. Satan has a strategy to take you out. You need a strategy to take him out. Pray and ask God, "Lord, show me the strategy," then listen. I tell people: You will know that what

you are hearing is from God when it's not something you would come up with, and it lines up with Scripture.

GROUP DISCUSSION QUESTIONS

1. We are in a battle. How do we fight this battle? If you had to explain to a new Christian how to engage in the battle, what would you say?

2. Why does the enemy come into your life?

3. What areas of your life has the enemy destroyed? Where do you need a resurrection?

4. What do you think Paul meant in Ephesians when he said that we need to be aware of our enemy's schemes? How can you better understand Satan's strategy to pull you away from God and the life He has for you? How might being aware of it help you to fight against it?

ELEVEN

Know Jesus
and Make Him Known

We are getting close to the end of this book, and there are two important questions you need to answer:

1. Why do you want a miracle?
2. What if you don't get one?

So, the miracle you are praying for: Why do you want it? What is motivating you to pray for it? And what if it doesn't come through? (We will address that last question in the next chapter.)

What If the Answer Is "I Never Knew You"?

To position yourself for a miracle, you need to know Jesus.

You need to *know Jesus*, not know *about Jesus*.

When Jesus was walking on the earth, the people who should have known Him best were those from His hometown. They had known Jesus His entire life. They could show you the house He grew up in, tell you about His parents, share stories of what He did as a toddler and what He was like as a teenager. But it turns out they knew all about Jesus but didn't know Jesus.

> Jesus left there and went to his hometown, accompanied by his disciples. When the Sabbath came, he began to teach in the synagogue, and many who heard him were amazed.
>
> "Where did this man get these things?" they asked. "What's this wisdom that has been given him? What are these remarkable miracles he is performing? Isn't this the carpenter? Isn't this Mary's son and the brother of James, Joseph, Judas and Simon? Aren't his sisters here with us?" And they took offense at him.
>
> Jesus said to them, "A prophet is not without honor except in his own town, among his relatives and in his own home." He could not do any miracles there, except lay his hands on a few sick people and heal them. He was amazed at their lack of faith.
>
> Mark 6:1–6

They were not positioned for a miracle because they didn't know Jesus. They knew more about Him than anyone, but they didn't know Him in a personal way that produced real faith.

I'm afraid we would find the same thing to be true in too many churches today. So many people know about Jesus. They could tell you stories about Him from the Bible and maybe even some good theology; but they don't know Jesus in a personal way that produces real faith.

I have some sports-crazy friends who can tell you everything about their favorite athletes. They know their personal backgrounds, their career statistics, even details of their private lives. They know all about their favorite sports stars—but they don't know them. Right? If they approached American sports greats LeBron James, Steph Curry or Tom Brady, my friends would say hi and excitedly tell all the facts they know. But LeBron or Steph or Tom would look confused and say, "Sorry, I don't know you."

Jesus tells us that a day is coming when people will approach Him, excited, assuming they are about to get into heaven, but He will tell them, "I never knew you" (Matthew 7:23). What Jesus wants is not someone who can recite facts about Him, but someone who loves Him and has a personal relationship with Him. What He wants with you is a love relationship.

When you know Jesus, you are positioning yourself for a miracle; when you don't know Jesus, you are not. In Acts 19:13–16 we read about some people who know about Jesus and try using His name in order to do a miracle: cast a demon out of a guy.

But instead the demon says, "Jesus I know . . . but who are you?"

Then the demon-possessed man "gave them such a beating that they ran out of the house naked and bleeding."

Looks as though the choice is this: Know Jesus and be positioned for a miracle or not know Jesus and end up naked and bleeding. I choose knowing Jesus!

Know Jesus More

I choose knowing Jesus, and I want to know Jesus more! Don't you? I know and love Jesus, but there is so much more to know and love.

So back to the first question: Why do you want a miracle?

To know Jesus more is, in my opinion, one of the two best answers you and I can give.

James tells us, "You don't have what you want because you don't ask God for it. And even when you ask, you don't get it because your motives are all wrong—you want only what will give you pleasure" (James 4:2–3 NLT).

Our motive for asking is a big deal. James says we will not receive what we ask for if we ask for it just wanting pleasure. "It will make me happy" is not a valid reason to ask for a miracle. "I want to know Jesus more" is a great reason to ask for a miracle. And when God breaks through and does a miracle in our lives, we often experience and come to know Him in a new and even more profound way.

Something we should consider, then, is this: Are we seeking God's face or seeking God's hand? God's hand speaks of His reaching down and intervening in our lives. Seeking God's hand indicates that we want Him to do something for us.

God's face signifies who He is. Seeking God's face means we want Him.

We all want to be happy. Who wouldn't desire a better job or a loving marriage or to be in better health or for that annoying neighbor to move away? We want to be happier. That's not necessarily wrong, but I believe there is something we really want, and it goes deeper than happiness. We want joy, an abiding sense of contentment. Joy is not based on our circumstances; it can be found only in God. Jesus taught repeatedly that we need to seek God. We shouldn't seek things we think will make us happy; we should seek God. When we have Him, when we know Him, we obtain something much better than happiness.

I think some people believe in God and have Him in their lives, but they still don't understand that He is what they truly want. So instead of seeking more of Him, they ask Him to bless them with the things they think will make them happy. There is actually something in us that seeks happiness—and persists in seeking it in places other than God. We are fixated on our circumstances. We want God's blessings instead of wanting God. But the truth is that nothing less than God will satisfy us. Our wants are too small.

Anne Graham Lotz (daughter of Billy Graham) was interviewed about some difficult hardship she was going through. She said, "Don't give me sympathy. Don't give me advice. Don't even give me a miracle. Just give me Jesus."[1]

While I don't agree with "Don't even give me a miracle," I love her attitude. Our desire is for more of Jesus. When we ask God to "Please give me a miracle," it should be because we want to experience more of Him. We seek God's face, not just His hand.

I love how David asked God for this in the psalms. He wrote:

My heart says of you, "Seek his face!" Your face, Lord, I will seek (Psalm 27:8).

O God, you are my God, earnestly I seek you; my soul thirsts for you, my body longs for you, in a dry and weary land where there is no water (Psalm 63:1 NIV1984).

How long, O Lord? Will you forget me forever? How long will you hide your face from me? (Psalm 13:1 NIV1984).

David prayed for God to intervene in his circumstances just as we do; but more than wanting God to bless him, he wanted God. God's presence needs to be more important to us than God's presents.

If we value God for the things He does for us more than for who He is, we run into a certain danger: When we don't think God is giving us what we want, we will be disappointed and perhaps even drift away from Him. If what attracts me to God is what He can do for me, then when He isn't doing it, I can lose my attraction to Him.

Also, when we get to heaven, I think there is a sense in which the miracles that happened on earth won't matter. *You were healed of cancer? Cool! But you ended up dying and going to heaven anyway. God restored your marriage? Awesome! But either way you were going to die and go to heaven forever.* What will really matter when we move from this temporary life into eternity is this: Do we know Jesus? Or will He say, "I never knew you."

In eternity, the miracles will not really matter. How you knew and loved God will.

So ask for a miracle. Yes. But ask because you want to know Jesus more.

Make Jesus Known

The more you know Jesus, the more you want Jesus to be known. As Jesus becomes the desire of your heart, the desire of your heart becomes making Him the desire of everyone's heart.

Why do you want a miracle?

To make Jesus known is, in my opinion, the *other* best answer we can give.

You want to make Him known because you know that everyone needs to know Him.

You want to make Him known because you see God's lost children and know He wants to know them. He wants them to come home to Him.

Jesus told a story about a shepherd who had one hundred sheep. One hundred sounds like a lot of sheep to me. One sheep wandered away. The shepherd now had 99 sheep. That still sounds like a lot of sheep, more than enough, to me.

Not in the mind of this shepherd. He left the 99 to go out in pursuit of the one lost sheep. He would do anything he had to do to get that sheep back. When he finally found it, Jesus said he put the sheep on his shoulders to carry it home.

My shoulders are the last place I want a sheep. This shepherd didn't seem to mind. In fact, when he got home he pulled out his cell phone and called all his family and friends, inviting them to a party to celebrate the safe return of his lost sheep. A celebration seems a bit much for a sheep, but not in the mind of this shepherd. He and his friends rejoiced at the return of the wandering sheep.

It's all about carrying people to Jesus.

Why? Because the shepherd in the story represents God, and the sheep represents your neighbor, your coworker, your friend, your family member who doesn't know Jesus.

God is willing to do anything to pursue His lost children and get them home to Him. He will do anything including miracles.

Doubting Thomas

Throughout the Bible, miracles are often called "signs." Miracles are signs the Holy Spirit uses to point people to Jesus. Jesus Himself used miracles to help people who were drifting from their faith.

Thomas is one of Jesus' Twelve. He has been with Jesus for three years, hearing Jesus' teaching and witnessing His miracles. Then Jesus is arrested and crucified. The disciples watch Jesus die, and as the blood drains from His body, the faith drains from their hearts. Jesus warned them this would happen, but they didn't listen. Now, watching Him be humiliated and executed is just too much. Their best friend suffers right in front of their eyes. Thomas tosses his faith and goes home.

Three days later reports start coming in that Jesus is alive. People have seen Him risen from the dead. Thomas hears about it but, unlike the other disciples, has not seen Jesus for himself. He does not believe. In fact, when the other disciples tell him they have seen Jesus, Thomas replies angrily, "Unless I see the nail marks in his hands and put my finger where the nails were, and put my hand into his side, I will not believe it" (John 20:25).

Soon Thomas finds himself in a house with the other disciples. The doors are locked, but suddenly Jesus appears. He breaks through into their presence supernaturally, and we discover that this miracle is a sign to help Thomas believe.

Jesus goes directly to Thomas and says, "Put your finger here; see my hands. Reach out your hand and put it into my side. Stop doubting and believe" (John 20:27).

The return of Thomas' faith is instantaneous. "Thomas said to him, 'My Lord and my God!'" (John 20:28).

Jesus explains that the reason for the miracle is to help Thomas get his faith back, and then He shares His desires for those not present in the room: "Jesus told him, 'Because you have seen me, you have believed; blessed are those who have not seen and yet have believed'" (John 20:29).

And, lest we miss the message that the chief purpose of miracles is to point people to Jesus in hopes that those who don't believe will believe, John next writes: "Jesus performed many other signs in the presence of his disciples, which are not recorded in this book. But these are written that you may believe that Jesus is the Messiah, the Son of God, and that by believing you may have life in his name" (John 20:30–31).

Miracles are signs that point people to Jesus that they might believe, and that, by believing, find life in Him.

That may be why today, when we see a tidal wave of miracles, it is usually in a place where evangelism is happening for the first time, where people are finally getting the chance to hear about and put their faith in Jesus. J. P. Moreland writes: "A major factor in the current revival in the Third World—by some estimates, up to seventy percent of it—is intimately connected to signs and wonders as expressions of the love of the Christian Father-God, the Lordship of His Son, and the power of His Spirit and

His Kingdom."[2] There are estimates that ninety percent of the amazing growth of the Church in China today is being fueled by healings. Edmond Tang at the University of Birmingham writes, "This is especially true in the countryside, where medical facilities are often inadequate or non-existent.[3]

Around the world today, countless Muslims have experienced supernatural visions or dreams that have brought them to Jesus. More Muslims have become Christians in the last few decades than in the previous fourteen hundred years since Muhammad. It is estimated that around thirty percent of them had a dream or vision of Jesus that began their journey to faith in Him.[4]

God is pursuing His lost children. If He has to break through the natural with the supernatural, He will do it.

God healing you is awesome. God restoring your broken relationship is awesome. God setting you free from an addiction is awesome. But when a miracle leads one of God's lost children home to Him? That's *awesome*.

The Real Significance

About ten months after God brought John Smith back from the dead, a twelve-year-old girl named Kassie was transferred from Branson, Missouri, to Children's Hospital in St. Louis. She had the flu, which had caused a stroke. She was in critical condition in the ICU when I received the call.

The voice on the phone said, "This is dire. We need a pastor."

I went and prayed for Kassie. I was thinking, *We had John, now we have this girl. This is the next miracle!* I did all the same things we did with John and waited for the good news.

Good news didn't come. The next day I was told, "She's not improving. She's actually getting worse."

The day after that, Kassie's condition was even worse. I arrived to find a man on his knees next to Kassie's bed. He was praying, crying out to God. I later learned that this was Kassie's father. He was not saved. He didn't go to church. I found out he was a rough dude who spent most of his nights getting into bar fights.

He got up off his knees and said, "God, I release her into Your hands. I know You can take care of her better than I can." He got down close to Kassie's head and whispered, "Honey, I'm okay. I have given my life back to Jesus."

Fifteen minutes after that point all of Kassie's numbers dropped. Her condition worsened; she wasn't turning around. She died that evening. I prayed. There was no resurrection.

I was so confused. *Lord, what's up? Why didn't You answer? We did all the right things to position ourselves for a miracle.*

I listened for God's answer and had the sense He was saying, *Just watch.* It seemed as though Kassie died without a purpose, but I felt that God was indicating there *was* a purpose.

I was asked to lead Kassie's funeral. More than a thousand people showed up from the community. The auditorium was filled with kids from her school that were rocked by Kassie's death. She was well loved. I presented the Gospel in my message and did an altar call. Hands went up all over the room.

After the funeral, the children's minister of the church told me that Kassie had prayed every Wednesday night for three years for her father to come to faith. Every week she came to church and prayed, "God, whatever it takes, bring my dad back to You." In the hospital, next to Kassie's bed, her father gave his life to Jesus. He spoke at the funeral and shared his new faith in God. He was a new man. I cannot imagine how difficult it must have been for him to get up and share hope with everyone in the room. He's my hero.

Could God have saved Kassie or raised her up after she died? Yes. But if her death somehow led to her dad knowing Jesus, her dying was a better miracle than saving her from death would have been. Right? After all, the difference between Kassie dying at twelve or several decades later is really not significant in light of her spending all of eternity in heaven. But the difference between her father knowing or not knowing Jesus? In light of eternity, that is completely significant.

This life is just a breath. None of us gets out of here alive. We are all going to die. What matters is what happens to us after we die.

A ministry friend of mine told me about his first experience with someone dying when he was just starting out as a new pastor. Meghan was sixteen years old. She was driving home one Saturday night from bowling with some friends when she swerved off the road and ran into a light pole. My friend got the call about midnight.

He could not understand it. Meghan and her parents knew Jesus. Knowing Jesus positions you for a miracle. Why hadn't God prevented Meghan's car from swerving? Why didn't God protect her when she hit the pole? Why didn't He bring her back to life?

He was even more confused because Meghan and her parents were very evangelistic. They were always sharing their faith and inviting people to church. One of Meghan's frustrations was that most of her high school friends wouldn't come to faith or to church with her. Now that she was gone, how would those teenagers hear about Jesus? How would they ever come to know Him?

He prayed but got no answer. So he focused on preparing his first funeral message.

At the funeral, my friend shared Meghan's love for God, and God's love for His lost children. He explained that while grieving for Meghan was appropriate, they could grieve with hope, because to be absent from the body is to be present with God. Meghan was in the loving arms of God, and that is where

Meghan had always wanted to be. He said that is where God wants everyone, because we are all His kids, and God is always pursuing His lost children and inviting them home to His loving embrace.

After the funeral, eight of Meghan's friends asked Meghan's dad to take them to the beach and baptize them. Eight people whom Meghan desperately wanted to know Jesus came to know Jesus through her death. Meghan had tried but could not figure out how to point her friends to Jesus. God knew how.

I am not saying God caused Meghan's death, but I am saying that God brings good out of all things for those who love Him. And I am saying that the greatest good is to know Jesus more and make Him known. We exist to love, serve and glorify God, and Meghan's eight friends are now living out the purposes for their lives on this earth and will someday live it out for all eternity in heaven.

Could God have saved Meghan or raised her up after she died? Yes. But if her death somehow led to her friends knowing Jesus, her dying was a better miracle than saving her from death would have been.

Why do you want the miracle you want?

The best reasons? To know Jesus more and to make Him known.

When that is your motive, you have positioned yourself for a miracle.

CONNECT WITH GOD

God, I truly want to know Jesus. Not just know about Him but know Him in a personal and intimate way. That will position me for a miracle—but more than a miracle, I want to know Jesus. I want to keep knowing Him more.

I want everyone to know Jesus. It breaks my heart that people are living without Him and that they will face eternity without Him. I know Your heart is for Your lost children. Father, I pray that everything I do, and everything You do for me, points people to Jesus. Purify my motives in asking for a miracle. Help me, more than anything else, to want people to see how amazing You are, and to want those people to put their faith in Your Son.

I thank You so much that I know Jesus. I pray in His name, Amen.

POSITION YOURSELF

1. Read the stories in the Bible where Jesus did miracles. How did those miracles help the person who experienced them know Jesus more? How did they help make Jesus known?

2. In chapter 1 you were asked: What miracle are you seeking? Now the important follow-up question: Why do you want the miracle you want? What's your motivation? Is it possible that your motives are all wrong—that you want only what will give you pleasure? Take some time to pray and ask the Holy Spirit to reveal your heart to you so you can discern your true motives. Ask God to purify your motives.

3. Think about that miracle you are seeking. If God were to grant it, how could it help you to know Jesus more? How could it help others to know Jesus? Do you maybe need to change the way you are praying for the miracle—to begin to focus on knowing Jesus more and making Jesus known?

GROUP DISCUSSION QUESTIONS

1. It is relatively easy to know about Jesus, but we need to know Him. How could you really get to know Jesus? If that became the priority of your life, how would your life change?

2. What is motivating you to pray for miracles in your life? Be honest: Why do you want the miracle you are praying for?

3. How do you think your desires would be different if you were seeking God's "face" more than God's "hand"?

4. Is making Jesus known a priority for you?

5. In what ways would the miracles you are praying for make Jesus known?

TWELVE

When God Doesn't Give You What You Want

Marj had brain cancer. She was in her fifties, had two children and a grandchild. She was a faithful follower of Jesus and an active member of a church pastored by a friend of mine—a church she had helped start. The congregation believed in God's ability to do miracles, and they prayed for one. They just knew a miracle was coming. It didn't. Marj's condition continued to deteriorate, then she died.

Why?

Why does God sometimes appear not to answer our prayers? At least the way we want Him to? Why does the miracle not happen?

The miracle not happening is not a new phenomenon. God has always been capable of doing miracles, but He has not always done the miracles people ask for, or done them the way that people expect Him to do them.

In the Old Testament, there's Job. Job loses all of his wealth and, worse, all of his children. Job is a godly man and certainly he has prayed for God's protection over his kids, his livestock, his property. God does not protect. Why?

In the New Testament, there's Mary and Martha. Their beloved brother, Lazarus, gets sick. They are friends with Jesus, so they send a message asking Him to come, to help, to heal their brother. Jesus doesn't show up. Lazarus dies. Why?

We still see this happen today.

I think of Douglas Groothuis, a Christian philosopher and professor. Douglas's wife, Rebecca, also a Christ-follower, was diagnosed with primary progressive aphasia. This disease robbed her of her ability to speak and think.[1] Douglas, Rebecca and their faith-filled friends prayed for healing, but God did not come through with a miracle. She died. Why?

I think of Nathan, a 34-year-old married man with two little kids. He showed up at our church, not a believer in Jesus. One Mother's Day, Nathan gave his life to Jesus. About a year later Nathan got melanoma cancer. He and his family prayed for healing. Our church prayed for healing. Nathan kept getting worse. Soon, he was barely holding on.

I sat with him in his hospital room and told him, "We're going to fight for you until you tell us you're ready to go home."

Nathan tried to smile. "I'm ready. I'm ready to go home and be with God."

I told the family, "You need to release him."

They were confused. "So, we're giving up? We're going to stop fighting?"

I assured them, "No, we still believe. We keep fighting. But he told us he's ready to go home. I think we need to tell him, and God, 'If you're ready to go home, we release you.'"

We did. We told Nathan. But we assured each other: If God wants to heal him, He can and will, and we will fight and believe for a miracle to the end. We weren't giving up. Nathan died soon after. When he did, I walked out of his room and cried. Why?

When God doesn't give us what we want, we want to know why. The problem is that we usually can't figure out why. *Why?* is a mystery. In the long run I'm glad that God doesn't answer the why many times. Figuring out the why doesn't help us.

Jerry Sittser is a believer and a professor at Whitworth University. Some years back, Jerry was driving with his mother, his wife and his daughter when their minivan was hit by a drunk driver. Jerry survived; everyone else died. In a moment, Jerry lost three generations of women in his family, three people he loved.

He replayed the scene a thousand times, asking all the *What if?* questions: "What if I had left ten seconds earlier?" "What if I had left ten seconds later?" "What if we had taken another route?" Then he started wrestling with all the *Why?* questions. "Why didn't God prevent the accident?" "Why did the drunk driver have to hit our car?" "Why me?"

Over time, he realized he would never be able to answer the *Why?* questions, and he gradually realized there was a much more important question facing him: How will I respond?

How Do *You* Respond?

How do you respond when God doesn't give you what you want? As a pastor, I have seen all kinds of people respond in all kinds of ways. Some of those ways are not healthy and further exacerbate the problems they are already experiencing.

How have you responded in the past when God didn't give you what you wanted?

How will you respond if it happens again in the future?

When I counsel people, I encourage them to . . .

Hang on to God

Philip Yancey is a Christian author who has written extensively on disappointment with God. The conclusion he comes to is this: In this life, we are going to experience disappointment. We can't avoid facing some circumstances where things don't go our way and our *Why?* questions are not answered. So, really, we have two options: We can be disappointed with God or we can be disappointed without God. We are going to be disappointed. Would you rather be disappointed with God, feeling that He has let you down but still hanging on to Him, or would you rather be disappointed alone, without God?

Steve was a longtime alcoholic and new follower of Jesus. For a while he was willing to live a double life. Eventually it led, as you might expect, to his hitting rock bottom. Finally, Steve realized he had to give up his drinking. He told God, prayed and stopped drinking. He assumed that he would no longer be tempted to drink. He prayed he would no longer be tempted to drink. He continued to be tempted to drink. Every day he wanted desperately to drink, so every day he depended desperately on God to help him make it through the day sober. Each night he would spend a long time begging God to take away the temptation, and then he would spend the entire next day being tempted and radically leaning on God to get him through.

He kept asking, "Why? Why isn't God taking away the temptation?"

Then it finally hit him: He didn't want God to take away the temptation. The temptation was forcing him to hang on to God. He was disappointed God had not taken it away, but every day God did not take it away was a day when he was forced to rely on God—and experience growing intimacy with Him.

Remember Douglas and Rebecca Groothuis? Before her death, as they continued to pray for healing, Douglas responded this way: "I'm hanging by a thread. But, fortunately, the thread is knit by God."

Remember Jerry Sittser? His mother, wife and young daughter all died in the minivan he was driving. He wrote a book about journeying with God through the pain. I love the title of the book. It's called *A Grace Disguised*.[2] Sittser writes that when we are desperate and disappointed with God we have an opportunity to experience God's presence and love in a way we never have before. Our disappointments are actually a grace disguised.

Give God the Benefit of the Doubt

How do guys like Steve and Douglas and Jerry hang on to God when they are disappointed with God? I think they are able to do that because they have already decided what they believe about God.

Think about that: People are able to trust God, even when He isn't giving them what they want, because they have already decided what they believe about Him. In these desperate moments, they are not just now deciding what they believe about God. They have spent their lives getting to know God, through reading the Scriptures, through prayer, through God providing, through personal experience—they have a real relationship with God. They know Him to be good. Then in extreme difficulties, they don't go by the way they feel or what they are seeing, but what they know. They know God.

When you have already decided that you can trust God, you are able to give Him the benefit of the doubt when you have doubts.

I am not saying you will necessarily understand God and what He is doing. Even so, you will be able to trust Him because you have already settled the question of His character. You may have doubts, but you will give God the benefit of the doubt.

I bet you have people in your life to whom you give the benefit of the doubt. Let's say you are supposed to meet a friend for lunch. You are sitting in the restaurant, by yourself. Your friend hasn't shown up.

There are some people about whom you'd be thinking, *My friend is so flaky!* or *That insensitive jerk!* But you also have reliable friends. Friends who have proven their character and never let you down. If one of those friends failed to show up, you would be concerned. *This isn't like her. I hope nothing happened. Maybe there was a car accident.*

You wouldn't assume the worst about your friend's character; you would assume the best. You might have doubts, but you would give this friend the benefit of the doubt. Why? Because you know your friend. You have already decided that this friend is trustworthy.

The same is true of God. I have come to realize that the best time for me to decide what my attitude toward God is going to be is not when I am in the middle of some painful situation. The best time to consider God's character is when I have a clear head and can make an honest evaluation.

What I know is that God is love, that God is for me and that God was willing to do the hardest thing possible (have His Son die) for me. I know that God is powerful, He is on my side and He is working in my situation even when I can't see it. This all tells me there is nothing He would not do for me.

When God doesn't give you what you want, you remember who He is. You may not know the why, but you know that He knows, and you know Him.

Know You Are in the Middle of the Story

When you hang on to God and give Him the benefit of the doubt, you understand that He has not finished yet. He is still working. Your circumstances feel all wrong, but you realize that you are only in the middle of the story.

Think about some of the stories we have looked at from the Bible where Jesus did miracles. We have the benefit of reading about those times after the fact. When people were walking through those stories, they didn't have the Bible to read and would have had no idea what the outcome was going to be. They had to walk by faith.

The hosts of the banquet were likely freaking out because the wine had run out at the wedding. They knew this was a humiliation they would never live down.

The woman who had been unable to stop bleeding for over a decade had tried every doctor, every remedy, and nothing worked. It seemed she would be sick forever.

Jairus had a daughter who died while Jesus healed and then had a conversation with some random woman. His heart shattered.

The disciples were caught in the perfect storm and were sure they were going to drown.

What did they all have in common? They were all losing it and were wrecked emotionally.

What else did they all have in common? They were all in the middle of the story. They thought their stories were over, that things couldn't change—but no, they were only in the middle of the story.

The same is true for us. When we pray and ask God for something, He doesn't always give us what we want, when we want it. But He always gives us what we need, when we need it.

I know that for me, some of the times I felt the most desperate were also the times I was the most certain God wasn't doing anything. I now look back and realize that those were the times God was totally doing something in my life; I just couldn't see it yet. I was still in the middle of the story.

When we are in the middle of the story, we don't have all the facts yet. We think we do, but we don't. We have no idea what God is doing. We don't know why God is not doing what He is not doing. Since we don't have all the facts, we need to have faith.

If you are losing it or wrecked emotionally, you need to realize you don't have all the facts. You are still in the middle of the story.

Remember Mary and Martha? In John 11 we read how their brother, Lazarus, is dying so they send a message to Jesus. Jesus does not show up in time. Lazarus dies. They are wrecked. What they don't know is that they don't know. They think they have all the facts, but they don't.

Jesus shows up and Mary and Martha both hit Him with an accusing statement: "Lord, if only You had been here, my brother would not have died."

Jesus seeks to speak life into Martha's faith, saying, "I am the resurrection and the life. The one who believes in Me will live, even though he dies; and whoever lives by believing in Me will never die. Do you believe this?"

When Jesus sees Mary and others weeping over the loss of Lazarus, He cries with them. (I love that. When we hurt, even though God knows our emotions are based on feelings, not on facts, He still hurts with us.)

It seems like the end of the story except . . . not so fast.

Jesus asks to be taken to the grave.

Then He prays: "Father, I thank You that You have heard Me. I knew that You always hear Me, but I said this for the benefit of the people standing here, that they may believe that You sent Me."

See the purpose of the miracle? The miracle is to help people know Jesus and make Jesus known.

Next, Jesus calls Lazarus—and he comes walking out of the grave! He is alive again. Talk about speaking life!

Mary and Martha think it is the end of their story. Jesus shows up, but He is way too late. His timing is all wrong.

No. Jesus has perfect timing. He comes when Lazarus had been dead four days. Back then there was some belief that a person's spirit hung around the body for three days after death, but after four days his or her story was totally over. The miracle is more amazing to everyone because Jesus does it on the fourth day. Jesus' timing brings God more glory. It proves that Jesus is who He says He is, and can do what He says He can do.

They thought Jesus had let them down, but they were in the middle of the story.

John Goldingay is a seminary professor. His wife, Anne, got MS and though they prayed for a miracle, it did not come. John wrote about her physical suffering and his disappointment in a very faith-filled book called *Walk On*.[3] Goldingay helps us with the *Why?* questions, saying, "There may sometimes be explanations for calamity that we do not know. But we have to live with God without knowing them." So how does he suggest we walk on with God? "We are invited to name our hopelessness and to let ourselves be soaked, enfolded, immersed in the counter-story of Jesus' life, death, and resurrection, because they are the basis for hope."[4]

He is saying we need to understand and embrace the whole story. Jesus' story is our story. He lived, then died, then rose from the dead. Unanswered prayer in a garden and from a cross was the middle of the story. Death was the middle of the story. Three days of silence was the middle of the story. Resurrection was still coming.

When God does not give you what you want, remember that you are still in the middle of the story, and the middle often has unanswered prayers and death and silence.

You might be struggling with that. Does every story really have a great ending?

I think so. And to understand the great ending we have coming, we need to focus on the middle of Jesus' story.

When Jesus was dying, everyone would have thought the best miracle would be God saving Him from the cross. Except that is the worst thing that could have happened. Temporarily it might have been good, but eternally His being saved would have meant no one else could be. We are saved because He wasn't. A "miracle" of Jesus triumphing over the cross without dying would have meant no triumph over the cross after dying. More life on earth as a human for Jesus would have meant eternal death for all us humans.

I bet people were watching Jesus die, praying that God would do a miracle and get Him off that cross alive. So can we agree that sometimes the best miracle is not getting the miracle we are praying for?

And can we agree that if we embrace that, we will finally understand that every story ends with a miracle?

In the End . . .

Remember my friend Nathan who died of cancer? We prayed for healing, but Nathan died. No miracle? Or was that just not the end of the story? If we are immersed in the counter-story of Jesus' life, death and resurrection, we realize that immediately after Nathan died, he was healed, and he walked through the door to new and eternal life.

Remember Marj, the lady in my pastor friend's church? She got brain cancer. The church prayed, but her condition got worse and she died. A couple months before she died, she shared her testimony at their church service. She said, "I'm praying that God will do a miracle and take away my cancer, but He's already done a greater miracle for me by taking away my sin. I already got the miracle. And so, if I die, I know where I'm going, and I've got no problem with that."

Marj died, but she died healed. Healed permanently of her brain cancer, and healed of her sin disease, and therefore able to spend eternity with the God she loved.

In the end, no one gets out of here alive. Lazarus was raised to new life, but Lazarus died again. John Smith was raised to new life, but some day John Smith is going to die again. We all die. But after this life there is life. There is life with God, with healing, without tears or sadness. In the end, there will be no more need for miracles. We will stop praying for God to break through into our world, because we will finally break through to His and to Him.

In the end, there is always a great ending.

CONNECT WITH GOD

Father God, there have been times when I have felt as though You weren't paying attention, as though You weren't showing up. I realize now that I didn't know all the facts; I just thought I did. My disappointment with You was probably more rooted in my pride than in what You were or weren't doing.

God, what I do know is who You are. You are love. You are good. You are a caring Father. I know that You are trustworthy, and I can trust You no matter what I am going through. Please help me to hang on. Please help me not to have doubts and, if I do, to give You the benefit of the doubt.

When things seem wrong, please remind me that it's just the middle of the story. Help me to immerse myself in Jesus' counter-story of life, death and resurrection. Let me never lose hope. I know that because my sins are forgiven, my story will end with the ultimate miracle as You heal me and bring me to be with You forever in heaven.

I pray in Jesus' powerful name, Amen.

POSITION YOURSELF

1. Read Mark 15–16. How does the crucifixion seem to be the ending, a horrible ending, to the story? Why do you think people lost hope when Jesus died? What would have changed in their thinking if they had known what would happen three days later? How does the resurrection change the story and give the kind of ending everyone would have hoped for?

2. Think about some of the bad things you have gone through in the past. When your circumstances were challenging, did you feel as if the story was over? What did God end up doing with the hardship you went through? Did you learn from it? Grow from it? Get closer to Him through it? Did you learn that you can trust God and give Him the benefit of the doubt?

3. The book is over. Do you feel as though you have learned how to position yourself for God to break through and give you the miracle you need? Skim back through the chapters and create the strategy you will follow from now on to position yourself for a miracle.

GROUP DISCUSSION QUESTIONS

1. When God doesn't give you what you want, instead of asking "Why?" how could you focus on asking "How do I respond?" and "What does God want me to get out of this experience?"

2. In what areas of your life have you experienced disappointment? How did you process it?

3. When you look back at your life, have you grown more through hard times or good times? If hard times, is it possible the hard times were the good times?

4. How can you start to give God the benefit of the doubt?

5. In what ways have you allowed the enemy to lie to you and convince you that God is not good and doesn't care? Ask God to reveal the truth to you.

Afterword

A Word from Joyce Smith

Life is a choice.

I am not talking about women's rights; I am talking about how God gives us free will to choose things. That includes choosing or not choosing Him to be in our lives. We were created with a "divine DNA" that can only be satisfied and function correctly in relationship with our creator. Many of us go throughout our lives making choices to fill that "divine DNA" with everything else but what it was created to possess, propelling us into an endless search for wholeness. I tell my son all the time: "Every day you are confronted with choices: Good choices have good consequences; bad choices have bad consequences." It is how life works, and there are no exceptions. Scripture backs that up, for what you sow, you also will reap (see Galatians 6:7–9). Or to put it in today's terms, what goes around comes around.

I was blessed to be brought up in a home that believed in God and His miraculous wonder-working power. I witnessed it at a very early age attending an Oral Roberts tent meeting. (That statement will quickly age me.) I spent many a night on a quilt spread on a sawdust floor, under a tent, hearing the miraculous preached, followed by watching the miraculous come to pass. I have seen blind eyes opened, the lame walk, the deaf hear and many give their lives to the Lord. I wish I could tell you that this experience set in stone that I would always choose to follow God and His calling. Sadly, it did not. In my teens, as many teens do, I thought I became wise beyond my parents' years and experience. I was sure they were old and stupid, and that they just were not as wise and up to date as I. (Am I talking to anyone here, or am I the only one who experienced this phase?) That choice and mindset caused me to walk into the gates of hell across hot coals for ten years, destroying my life beyond what I thought could ever be restored. This is where the power of community prayer changes things. I had praying parents and friends who interceded for me, and when I was on the verge of suicide, God came in with grace and mercy, and I surrendered myself to Him.

God had a purpose for my life that He was weaving together, an amazing tapestry that would lead me on a journey I could never have believed possible—a journey of restoration and miracles. He was putting together a miraculous story beyond anything people would dream of. I was blessed with having a firm foundation of seeing miracles at an early age. I never questioned God's ability to do the miraculous; I had witnessed it firsthand. I was also blessed to be brought up in a fellowship of believers, with a pastor and his wife who walked what they taught. The foundation that was established through that nineteen-year tutelage would serve me well in developing an unshakable faith in God. There was an old hymn we used to sing called "Every Promise in the Book Is Mine." I would go on to find out the solid truth of that hymn as God brought me through the next thirty-plus years. God would restore my home and family. He supplied all of our needs. He restored my happiness. He gave us a son by adoption that would heal our family dynamics. . . .

I was happy and content, but I had no idea that God was up to something much more profound and amazing. The journey was just about to get more interesting and exciting.

The truths of God's promises are seen throughout the Bible. The promise of a Savior comes in chapter 3 of Genesis, and throughout the Old Testament we see the prophecy of the Messiah who is to come. In the second chapter of Luke in the New Testament we see that promise fulfilled.

In Genesis 12 God calls Abram to leave his home and follow God with no destination in mind, other than to follow God in blind faith. As you journey on with Abram and his family you see much adversity happening to him, yet he is obedient and does as God asks him without question. Was he perfect? No, he was not—but he was quick to obey. God honored Abram and changed his name to carry the breath of God. He became Abraham the father of the Jewish nation; a promise God fulfilled and honors to this very day.

It was stories like this that began to grip my curiosity about six years ago. Why did God call Abraham His friend? Why was God so faithful to Abraham and his descendants? Why did Mary, the mother of Jesus, find so much favor with God? Why was John so beloved by Jesus, and why was he not martyred as were the rest of Jesus' disciples? These and many other questions needed an answer.

I was reading our church bulletin one Sunday morning and noticed that a couple of friends of mine, Melissa Fischer and Keri Munholand, who would later become a very integral part of my inner circle, were having a Bible study on Wednesday mornings. That Bible study would profoundly change my life. The study was Beth Moore's book *The Patriarchs*. That was exactly what I was looking for to answer the whys that had gripped me. I loved every moment of those studies. I had learned many of the Bible stories as a child, yet now they were taking on new meaning. As the years went on I drank in those Bible studies as if I were in the desert thirsting and could not get enough water. I was becoming fortified as never before, fed by manna that was nourishing my soul like nothing I had ever experienced.

I didn't know I was being honed for a battle such as I had never ever experienced in my life. I was being delivered from control issues that haunted me. God knew in a short while only He could be in control of the situation I would face. God was fortifying me with His words, His promises, His truth and His faithfulness for a miracle He was going to use as His tool to share a miraculous story with the world. God never calls us to a purpose for which He has not already made provision. I was learning that God's faithfulness was not His job; it was His divine DNA. It is who He is.

Two years of God's preparation would bring me to the foot of a hospital bed where my son, who had drowned, was lying in front of me. He had been dead for over an hour. He was lifeless.

Now what was going to be my "go to" solution for this circumstance?

It was no coincidence that at that very time our group was using another Beth Moore Bible study called *Believing God*. As part of the daily material, we were encouraged to repeat our belief that God is who He says He is and can do what He says He can do, as well as the personal belief that I am who God says I am.

Now, it was time to use the tools God had given me to prepare me for this very moment in time. He had prepared me for this moment throughout my life with His faithfulness. Now it was show time.

I grabbed John's cold dead feet and this divine thought ran through my head: *God, either You are who You said You are or You are not.* I remembered Romans 1:4 that speaks of the power of the Holy Spirit who raised Christ Jesus from the dead. So, in a very loud voice, I cried out for the entire ER area to hear, "Holy Spirit, I need you right now to come and breathe life back into my son!"

A nurse would later tell us that at that very moment something so powerful touched John's body that she could hardly continue standing there. One of the individuals involved with performing CPR said the same. Both felt the mighty power of the Holy Spirit moving up John's body restoring his heartbeat.

God was faithful to honor my request. Within seconds I heard, "We have a heartbeat, we have a heartbeat!"

Everything they had done prior to that moment had failed. But now God was saying, *Stand back and watch. I am the God of the impossible. I am faithful and can be trusted.*

John walked out of the hospital sixteen days later, totally healed by the miraculous power of God.

What we have learned through this experience is the importance of positioning ourselves to believe for a miracle. The lessons Jason shares with you are the lessons God brought into focus as we prayed and believed God for a miracle in John's situation.

I want to encourage you today: If you are facing an impossible situation, take the teaching points from this book and use them to position yourself to be a conduit that God can work through to do incredible miracles.

If the Idea of a Relationship with God Is New to You

In the first chapter I asked: What miracle are you seeking?

Typically, people answer that question by talking about a physical condition, relational breakdown, addiction or troubling circumstance.

I get it. I have some of those, too.

But none of those is the greatest miracle you or I need. Our biggest problem is sin. Each of us has chosen to rebel against God. The Bible tells us in Romans 3:23 (NLT): "Everyone has sinned; we all fall short of God's glorious standard."

The problem is when we sin, we are telling God we don't want Him and don't want to do life His way. Sin also makes us guilty and deserving of punishment. It causes us to be lost. Trying to stumble through the dark in this life.

All of that is really a problem because we were made for a relationship with God. We were made to love God and live in His love—not just in this life, but for all eternity in a perfect place called heaven. But because we have sinned, we are separated from God and His love, and after this life we will be completely separated from God for all eternity.

So, what miracle should we be seeking most? A way of taking our sin away so we can have life with God.

Here is a surprise: Our sin is not just a problem for us; it is also a problem for God. It is a problem for God because despite our rebellion against Him, He still loves us. He still wants to be in relationship with us.

So God, in His great love for us, provided a way for our sins to be taken away so we can have life with Him. We are told in Romans 6:23 (NLT): "The wages of sin is death, but the free gift of God is eternal life through Christ Jesus our Lord."

Wages are something you earn. Our sin has earned us death.

A gift is something you are given that you haven't earned. God has offered us the gift of eternal life with Him through Jesus.

How? Through what I vote for as the greatest miracle of all: Jesus died on a cross, and because He was sinless, His death has the supernatural power to take your sins away.

Throughout this book we have read stories from the Bible of Jesus healing people with physical diseases. We have learned that Jesus heals. Our biggest problem is our sin disease, and Jesus came to heal it.

J.R.R. Tolkien, author of *The Lord of the Rings* series, was a Christian and loved the idea that God is a healer. He used lots of biblical imagery in his writing, often using the imagery of scars, such as the wounds Frodo and Gollum had from carrying the ring. Repeatedly he presented the idea of a wound that needs healing.

I love this line: "For it is said in old lore: *The hands of the king are the hands of a healer. And so the rightful king could ever be known.'"

Tolkien writes about how in the ancient world it was thought that kings had the ability to heal, always because of their power.

Jesus came to earth. He was the King of kings. He had the ability to heal. In a sense it was because He had power. But the strange and amazing thing is that Jesus chose to heal us of our greatest problem not through power but through weakness. We are told of Jesus in Isaiah 53:5 (NLT): "He was pierced for our rebellion, crushed for our sins. He was beaten so we could be whole. He was whipped so we could be healed."

We have seen Jesus heal people by reaching out His hands and touching them. The hands of this King were the hands of a healer. But for His most amazing miracle, Jesus had His hands nailed to a cross. It looked as though the healing power of His hands was being taken away, but no. Jesus allowed Himself to be nailed to a cross, and that act of weakness released the greatest healing power in the universe because His death can take away your sin. In fact, the Bible says that Jesus died for you and me while we were *still lost* in sin.

A gift is something offered to you, and God has offered you the gift of taking your sin and giving you abundant life now and then eternal life with Him in heaven. He has offered that gift; you have to accept it. You have to say yes.

How do you say yes?

You put your faith in Jesus and what He did on the cross for you. You tell God that you want a relationship with Him. You acknowledge that you have sinned, and that your sin separates you from Him. You accept Jesus as your Savior, as the only one who can save you from your sin by offering you forgiveness through what He did on the cross. You choose Jesus as your Lord; the one you want to lead you through the rest of your life.

When you put your faith in Jesus, another miracle happens: God moves inside of you. God is serious about having a relationship with you. He wants to be with you, and if you invite

Him in, He literally moves in, through the Holy Spirit. The Holy Spirit is God's presence and power in the lives of people who say yes. The Holy Spirit is in you so you are never alone, and He will guide and empower you into the life God has for you.

Don't you want all that? Don't you want to be forgiven of your sins, freed from your guilt, brought into relationship with God, given life with Him and filled with the Holy Spirit so God is in you empowering and leading you into the abundant and eternal life He has for you?

You can have it. You can have it right now. Here is a prayer you could pray telling God you accept His offer:

God, thank You so much for loving me.

I have done a really bad job of loving You. In fact, I realize I have spent most of my life running from You and sinning against You.

It's amazing to me that You still love me, and that You sent Jesus for me, and that Jesus was willing to die for me. Thank You. I could never thank You enough.

God, I accept Jesus' sacrifice for my sins. Please forgive me through what Jesus did for me.

God, I ask Jesus to be my Savior and I want Him to be my Lord, my leader. Jesus, please lead me through this life, and into heaven when I die. Please help me to follow You.

And God, thank You for giving me Your Holy Spirit. What a miracle that You want to live in me and help me to know You more and to live the life You have for me!

God, I accept Your offer. I invite You in. I give my life to You.

I know I can only do this because of Jesus and what He did on the cross for me.

I pray in His name, Amen.

The Breakthrough Prayer

BY DEVON FRANKLIN

Holy Spirit, breathe life back into my home;
Holy Spirit, breathe life back into my relationships;
Holy Spirit, breathe life back into my dreams;
Holy Spirit, breathe life back into my finances;
Holy Spirit, breathe life back into my family;
Holy Spirit, breathe life back into my church;
Holy Spirit, breathe life back into my life.
In the mighty name of Jesus, Amen!

If you prayed this prayer, life is being restored in you right now. Your breakthrough is on the way!

Notes

Chapter 1 God Still Breaks Through

1. Craig Groeschel, *The Christian Atheist: Believing in God but Living as if He Doesn't Exist* (Grand Rapids, Mich.: Zondervan, 2011).
2. Stanley Hauerwas and William H. Willimon, "Embarrassed by God's Presence," *Christian Century*, January 30, 1985, 100.
3. See, for instance, Acts 2:42–47 and Acts 4:32–35.
4. C. S. Lewis, *Miracles*, rev. ed. (San Francisco: HarperOne, 2015).
5. Craig S. Keener, *Miracles: The Credibility of the New Testament Accounts* (Grand Rapids, Mich.: Baker Academic, 2011).
6. Eric Metaxas, *Miracles* (New York: Penguin Books, 2015), 23.
7. Lee Strobel, *The Case for Miracles* (Grand Rapids, Mich.: Zondervan, 2018).
8. To read the full story of John being raised from the dead, and all the miraculous events around it, see Joyce Smith's book, *The Impossible* (FaithWords, 2017), also now the major motion picture, *Breakthrough*.

Chapter 2 Play Your Part

1. Actually it was more than five thousand people. Back then, when attendance was taken, they counted only the men. That day there would have been many women and kids. The crowd probably numbered some fifteen thousand people.
2. Strobel, *Miracles*, 93.
3. See Chauncey W. Crandall IV, M.D., *Raising the Dead: A Doctor Encounters the Miraculous* (New York: FaithWords, 2010), 1–5.

Chapter 3 Get Close to Jesus

1. Look, for instance, at Proverbs 28:13, James 5:16 and 1 John 1:9.
2. Keener, *Miracles*, 1:431–32.

Chapter 4 Overcoming Fear

1. Strobel, *Miracles*, 84.

189

Chapter 5 Live Desperate

1. Joshua Piven and David Borgenicht, *The Worst-Case Scenario Survival Handbook* (San Francisco: Chronicle Books, 1999).
2. Kyle Idleman, *Don't Give Up: Faith That Gives You the Confidence to Keep Believing and the Courage to Keep Going* (Grand Rapids, Mich.: Baker Books, 2019).
3. Piven and Borgenicht, *Worst-Case Scenario*, 125.
4. Piven and Borgenicht, *Worst-Case Scenario*, 127.
5. Editor's note: Brian's emotive post has been edited for clarification.

Chapter 6 Believe Big, Pray Big

1. Richard Harvey, *70 Years of Miracles* (Beaverlodge, Alberta, Canada: Horizon House, 1977), 63–66.
2. See Harold P. Adolph, *Today's Decisions Tomorrow's Destiny* (Spooner, Wis.: White Birch, 2006), 48-49; Scott J. Kolbaba, M.D., *Physicians' Untold Stories* (North Charleston, S.C.: CreateSpace, 2016), 115–22.

Chapter 8 Surround Yourself

1. If you're wondering what happened with the job and houses, God totally came through. The guy who sold us the new house turned out to be a Christian and told us he would hold the house for us. The job with the denomination came through. We were never homeless. We ended up with a great job, in a great house, in God's great timing.

Chapter 9 Keep Your Eyes Open

1. Strobel, *The Case for Miracles*, 93.
2. Candy Gunther Brown, *Testing Prayer: Science and Healing* (Cambridge, Mass.: Harvard University Press, 2012), 214.

Chapter 11 Know Jesus and Make Him Known

1. Larry Crabb, *The Pressure's Off* (Colorado Springs, Col.: WaterBrook, 2012), 72.
2. J. P. Moreland, *Kingdom Triangle: Recover the Christian Mind, Renovate the Soul, Restore the Spirit's Power* (Grand Rapids, Mich.: Zondervan, 2007), 168.
3. Allan Anderson and Edmond Tang, eds., *Asian and Pentecostal: The Charismatic Face of Christianity in Asia*, rev. ed. (Eugene, Ore., Wipf & Stock, 2011), 391.
4. See Tom Doyle, *Dreams and Visions: Is Jesus Awakening the Muslim World?* (Nashville: Nelson, 2012), 127.

Chapter 12 When God Doesn't Give You What You Want

1. Douglas Groothuis, *Walking Through Twilight* (Downers Grove, Ill.: InterVarsity, 2017).
2. Jerry L. Sittser, *A Grace Disguised* (Grand Rapids, Mich.: Zondervan, 2004).
3. John Goldingay, *Walk On* (Grand Rapids, Mich.: Baker, 2002).
4. Quoted in Scot McKnight, *The Jesus Creed: Loving God, Loving Others* (Orleans, Mass.: Paraclete Press, 2004), 263.

Pastor Jason Noble has been a lead pastor for the past nine years, national director for children's ministries/Assemblies of God USA, and a children's pastor. He is passionate about reaching the lost and helping build up, encourage and equip the local church. Throughout his ministry he has seen hundreds of people saved and hundreds of miracles. He speaks at churches and conferences throughout the world. Jason and his wife, Paula, have been married for 23 years and have four kids: Avi, Ryan, Audree and Julia. They live in Medford, Oregon.

For further information or to contact Pastor Noble, please visit:

Facebook: www.facebook.com/revjasonnoble

Instagram: @jason.noble

Twitter: @revJasonNoble

Website: www.breakthroughbook.com